WITHDRAWN

DUKE UNIVERSITY PUBLICATIONS

. . . the other
harmony of prose . . .

PAULL FRANKLIN BAUM

...the other

harmony of prose...

an essay in English prose rhythm

DUKE UNIVERSITY PRESS

1952

THIS BOOK WAS PUBLISHED WITH THE
ASSISTANCE OF THE INCOME FROM THE

P. HUBER HANES FUND

PRINTED IN THE UNITED STATES OF AMERICA
BY THE SEEMAN PRINTERY, INC., DURHAM, N. C.

PREFACE

THE FOLLOWING essay was planned several years ago and laid aside. But recently I came upon a doctoral dissertation in which the author speaks with such confident scorn of prose rhythm as barely existing that I was encouraged to renew the attempt.

It is all very well to speak of "the nearly universal susceptibility to the effect of rich and powerful sound," or to say defensively, as Arnold felt obliged to say of the *grand manner*, that the presence or absence of prose rhythm can only be spiritually discerned. But the effort to penetrate further, to see just what these effects are, brings out the difficulties. English prosody has a history of some thousand years, yet many of the fundamentals are still in dispute; and the study of prose rhythm is only beginning.

My aim has been to submit in brief form some of the principles which seem to underlie the rhythms of our language. By a liberal, and even loose, interpretation of the concept of rhythm, and by seeking help wherever it could be found, I may have incurred two charges (apart from that of repetitiousness) which, in the circumstances, ought to be counted for righteousness. By illustrative examples and analysis of them in a variety of ways I have endeavored to explore the possibilities of the subject and, it may be, open the way to a fuller and better understanding of English prose rhythm.

P. F. B.

ACKNOWLEDGMENTS

Thanks are due to the following publishers for generous permission to quote from their copyrighted books:

Cambridge University Press, American Branch, for the passage on pp. 10 f. from *An Enquiry concerning the Principles of Natural Knowledge*, by A. N. Whitehead;

Harcourt, Brace and Company, for the passage on pp. 56 f. from *Portraits in Miniature*, by Lytton Strachey;

Henry Holt and Company, Inc., for the passage on pp. 61 ff. and 197 ff. from *English Prose Style*, by Herbert Read;

E. P. Dutton & Co., Inc., for the passage on pp. 64 ff. from *The Sea and the Jungle*, by H. M. Tomlinson;

Farrar, Straus and Young, Inc., for the passage on pp. 68 f. from *Trollope: a Commentary*, by Michael Sadleir, revised American edition, copyright 1947;

Doubleday & Company, Inc., for the passage on pp. 69 f. from *Don Fernando*, by W. Somerset Maughm;

Alfred A. Knopf, Inc., for the passage on pp. 130 f. from *A Room with a View*, by E. M. Forster;

Appleton-Century-Crofts, Inc., for the passage on p. 132 from *John Ruskin*, by David Larg;

The Macmillan Company, for the passage on p. 193 from *The Brook Kerith*, by George Moore;

Oxford University Press, Inc., for the passage on p. 196 from *A Saintsbury Miscellany*.

CONTENTS

. . . the other
harmony of prose . . .

I

Rhythm

Prolegomena—Varia

i

TO THE QUESTION: *What is art?* says Croce at the beginning of his *Breviario*, it may be jestingly replied—"ma non sarebbe una celia sciocca"—that art is what everyone knows it to be. The same high and intuitive position might be taken on the question: *What is rhythm?* In a similar vein Professor J. H. Scott opines: "The fact is that we are too familiar with rhythm to recognize it; we know it only in its absence."* Much earlier St. Augustine said about *time*: "Si nemo a me quaerat, scio; si quaerenti explicari velim, nescio" (*Conf.* xi, 17). Quite so; but it behooves the poor expositor to be both humble and pedestrian: he must even plod his weary way, and let ambition mock his useless toil.

ii

Two introductory observations are in order. First, on the 'origins' of rhythm. For the psychologist and the philosophical materialist the beginning of rhythm is in the senses of the body: the action of the heart, the throb of the pulse, breathing, the stride in walking, the movements of the dance. There is not only a rhythmic sensation in those members actively engaged, but there is also a corresponding rhythmic sense distributed through the

* P. 118. Full citations of technical works are to be found in the Bibliography.

whole nervous system. The common name for this is body rhythm. Thus muscular tension and release is the basis of rhythm, and whether the original cause or not, it is certainly an unmistakable accompaniment affording responsive satisfactions in the act of reading. On the other hand, for the philosophical idealist rhythm is a primary law of being, which manifests itself in all nature, animate and inanimate—therefore in man, both mind and body. Whichever view one holds, the primacy of rhythm remains.[1]

Second, there is the important distinction between rhythm as a concept and rhythm as a percept, or to use the older terms, between objective and subjective rhythm. The one exists in the phenomenal world outside ourselves: a series of drum taps or organ notes, or any pattern of sounds and silences mechanically produced. In some sense, it is an idea or an abstraction. "Of all objective experience . . . very little is left as pure and genuine sensory fact," say the psychologists.[2] But what concerns us is the apprehension of these external rhythms by the individual hearer; and at once we are confronted with the notorious unreliability of the senses, which are in nothing quite so deceptive as in the perception of intervals of time. It has been found by laboratory experiment that readers may be genuinely susceptible to temporal values without being at all conscious of them. They may pause without knowing it or think they pause when the instruments record no silence. In these and other ways they misapprehend or misinterpret the sounds of speech. But while the statistics of the laboratory are often valuable, what really matters for us are the rhythms of the inner ear—what the reader feels and how he thinks he reads, what the hearer feels and thinks he hears. "A mind and a machine," says Professor Thomson caustically, "apprehend things differently."

iii

A glance at the dictionaries will show how wide-ranging is the concept of rhythm.

The word is from a Greek root meaning 'flow.' The Greek *rhythmos* is defined as measured motion, time (Lat. *numerus*); proportion or symmetry of parts; arrangement, order; the state or condition of the soul, temper, disposition; the form or shape (of a thing); manner or fashion—as in Euripides' "What rhythm [kind] of slaughter?" And consider this, from the Glossary of *The Aristoxenian Theory of Musical Rhythm*: "Measure, proportion, symmetry, measured motion, measured time. The word was anciently applied to prose, architecture, and sculpture, as well as to poetry, music, and dancing. It was also used for the common objects of daily life, such as a well-fitting pair of boots. A *Rhythm* is a member of a period, or even a single foot. The arrangement of the relative time-values of the individual notes is also called rhythm." Here is indeed God's plenty—from the Greeks alone.

The earliest use of the word in English is in the sense of rimed verse, and the word was pronounced *rime*. This use continued through the seventeenth century. In fact, Dr. Johnson does not list the noun *rhythm*, but only the adjective *rhythmical*.

The *O.E.D.* has a definition of it for prosody, but otherwise, for language, does not get beyond "The measured flow of words and phrases"—apropos of which it quotes A. M. Bell, *The Principles of Speech*, 1863: "In every sentence, however uttered, there is a rhythm." In art, rhythm is: "Due correlation and interdependence of parts, producing a harmonious whole." Finally, for a general definition: "Movement marked by regulated succession of strong and weak elements, or of opposite or different conditions"; and quotes Hardy: "So do flux and reflux—the rhythm of change—alternate and persist in everything under the sky."

The *Century Dictionary* is more generous and more helpful. Its fourth and fifth definitions are as follows: "In *physics* and *physiol.*, succession of alternate and opposite or correlative states."

The longer astronomic rhythm, known as the earth's annual revolution, causes corresponding rhythms in vegetable and animal life; witness the blossoming and leafing of plants in the spring, the revival of insect activity at the same season, the periodic flights of migratory birds, the hibernating sleep of many vertebrates, and the thickened coats or the altered habits of others that do not hibernate.—John Fiske, *Cosmic Philos.* I, 307.

"In the *graphic* and *plastic* arts, a proper relation and interdependence to each other and to an artistic whole." These are preceded by what amounts to a discussion:

Movement in time, characterized by equality of measures and by alternation of tension (stress) and relaxation . . . by development [from the original sense] 'uniform movement, perceptible as such, and accordingly divisible into measures, the measures marked by the recurrence of stress.' . . . Although regularity and definiteness of rhythm are characteristic of all music, various influences tend to modify and obliterate its form. . . . Except in very rudimentary music, purely rhythmic accents are constantly superseded by accents belonging to figures and phrases—that is, to units of higher degree than measures. Indeed, in advancing from rudimentary to highly artistic music, rhythmic patterns become less and less apparent, though furnishing everywhere a firm and continuous groundwork.

. . . Theoretically, all spoken language possesses rhythm, but the name is distinctively given to that which is not too complicated to be easily perceived as such. Rhythm, so limited, is indispensable in metrical composition, but is regarded as inappropriate in prose, except in elevated style and in oratory, and even in these only in the way of vague suggestions, unless in certain passages of special character.

But for a dash of mystery the *Century* includes this from the *Encyclopaedia Britannica*, xix, 262: "Rhythm . . . is of course governed by law, but it is a law which transcends in subtlety the conscious art of the metrist, and is only caught by the poet in his most inspired moods." This is certainly pregnant of direction; for a law which is to be caught only by inspiration is anarchy for the uninspired. But the statement means, 'of course,' that when it was written nothing could be considered right or sound which was not defined in terms of a *law*, even at the price of compromise with a 'law' deriving from "inspired moods"; and it turns out, on a little investigation, to have been written by Watts-Dunton.

In the fourteenth edition of the *Britannica* the article on rhythm is devoted chiefly to music, but it offers us this (by E. E. Kellett) on prose rhythm: it is "not only in the balance of the sentence, but in the arrangement of the sentences in paragraphs and in the building up of paragraphs into chapters."

From the musical 'authorities' less is to be expected than from the dictionaries, for two good reasons. One, which is paramount, is that music is written now in bars, as verse is written in feet, and therefore the proper comparison is between music and verse, not music and prose. The other reason is that the musicians are plagued with the same uncertainty and vagueness; they are as helpless as the rest of us.

"The term 'rhythm,'" writes A. Eaglefield Hull, "is perhaps more promiscuously used than any other term in music." It shifts from the simple division into bars, which "may be said to be the *metre* of the tonal art," to "the arrangement of the bars into figures, phrases, and sentences." (Which looks like retro-borrowing.) "It often concerns itself with the musical rhyming of the phrases and sentences, especially in the more formal music of Haydn and Mozart, and it is always connected with the graded increase and decrease of tension in musical pitch." "Having regard to the great elemental nature of its general application in ordinary parlance, it should stand in music for the regular pulsing of the beats, in the sense in which Berlioz described it as 'the very life-blood of music'" (p. 170).

Larousse quotes Guéroult: "Le rhythme a surtout la propriété de frapper et de remuer; c'est la partie sensuelle de la musique."

Modern music has turned more and more to free rhythm and the principle of prose; or, as the *International Cyclopedia of Music and Musicians* puts it, "Rhythm has become more and more independent of its metrical guide posts." It tries to overcome the traditionary inelastic notation, runs right through the bar line, resorts to such signatures as $\frac{8}{8}\left(\frac{3}{8} + \frac{2}{8} + \frac{3}{8}\right)$ and $\frac{7}{4}\left(\frac{2}{8}\right)$, and even dispenses with the time signature altogether. (In this mingling of different 'times' it resembles ancient Greek music and meter in their logaœdic measures.) Hull gives an example (*Modern Harmony*, p. 179) in which the orchestra plays two groups of four thirty-second notes against two groups of eighth notes, while beneath are heard three quarter notes against four eighths.

The *Cyclopedia* just cited provides us with a perfect *reductio ad absurdum:* "Its [music's] life force is rhythm, which one may define as order in movement, a never-ending flow of motion which, through human experience, has become regulated in time patterns perceptible to the senses. . . . Rhythm moulds melody into a musical thought. Tone without rhythm is unintelligible. Rhythm without tone is a fundamental concept. . . ."

After this it is a pleasure to turn to Mr. Abdy Williams's *The Rhythm of Modern Music* (1909), which is all the more interesting for being somewhat heretical. Rhythm, he says (p. 20), "may be defined as the measuring of the Time occupied in the performance of certain of the Fine Arts in such a manner as to render the Art-material concerned intelligible and interesting to our artistic sense." From our limited sense of time-measurement arises "the need for the alternation of accented and unaccented sounds." "The accented sounds serve to divide the time occupied by the Art-material into definite portions," which are themselves arranged "in groups, corresponding to the Sentences of Prose, and the Verses of Poetry. Into such groups, called Rhythms, or Phrases, all Music is divided; and the words Rhythm and Phrase mean exactly the same thing" (p. 21). "Thus, two or more Rhythms [or phrases], . . . form a Period, and a complete composition consists of a number of Periods" (p. 23). The analogy with prose is not perfect, but suggestive, and may be taken for what it is worth, without following further the analysis of musical form.

But it is Mr. Williams's observations in his introductory chapter which I find most helpful.

Rhythm has two sides. The first, and most obvious, is
that in which the interest is centered on the individual notes,
which follow one another in some noticeable manner, in
some rhythmical figure, which awakens in us feelings of
energy, or pleasure or excitement. . . .

The other side of Rhythm is the more intellectual, the
less obvious; it is that in which the phrases are of unexpected
lengths, or are divided in some particular way, so that it
requires some mental effort on the part of the listener to
understand what the composer is aiming at. . . . No music
that aims at merely being a pleasant easy pastime can make
use of this side of Rhythm; only those who are in earnest
can use or appreciate it.

He goes on to speak of the prevalence of the four-bar
phrase and the pleasure for the cultivated listener in any
variation from this staple. But what must strike and
shock certain readers is the absence of any talk about
equal measures or equal durations of the mere bar measurement. No doubt he expects them and takes them for
granted, but the emphasis is on larger divisions and movements, which are precisely the things which interest the
student of prose.

Now lastly (in the present series) let us hear from
a scientist and philosopher:

A rhythm involves a pattern and to that extent is always
self-identical. But no rhythm can be a mere pattern; for
the rhythmic quality depends equally upon the differences
involved in each exhibition of the pattern. The essence of
rhythm is the fusion of sameness and novelty; so that the
whole never loses the essential unity of the pattern, while
the parts exhibit the contrast arising from the novelty of
their detail. A mere recurrence kills rhythm as surely as

does a mere confusion of differences. A crystal lacks rhythm from excess of pattern, while a fog is unrhythmic in that it exhibits a patternless confusion of detail. Again there are gradations of rhythm. The more perfect rhythm is built upon component rhythms. A subordinate part with crystalline excess of pattern or with foggy confusion weakens the rhythm. Thus every great rhythm presupposes lesser rhythms without which it could not be. (Whitehead, p. 198)

V

After these variations and vagaries, almost a patternless confusion, it is time to sharpen the focus on the special problem of prose rhythm.

I begin with Professor Elton's summing up because he was an avowed follower of Saintsbury and because his position is eccentric to the main business and may be left with a Saintsburian "point and pass."

If, then, we ask what are the elements of rhythm, that is, of law, order and recurrence, which are to be found in English prose amidst its infinite variety, they may be classified for the present into the following: First, those successions of feet, defined by the 'foot-scansion' and consisting of entire words, that may be grouped under such a principle as 'gradation.' Secondly, the bursts, shorter rather than longer, of actual metre, that is of verse-feet, which are not necessarily made up of entire words. Thirdly, the cadences, coming at the end of groups, clauses or sentences, and of recurrent but not of metrical type; yet having in common with metre the fact, that they also strike across the word-divisions. These cadences are partly classical in origin (*cursus*) or native; the former having been classified, the latter still awaiting full classification. All these elements of law and order must be present to the ear together. (pp. 157-58)

Now for the rigorists, who will haggle over time and stress, serious matters to be developed in the sequel. First there is Professor E. A. Sonnenschein, who retired in the early twenties to his "eyrie amid the Somersetshire hills," where "a new light seemed to dawn" and he found that his "bit of chaos" had "at last fashioned itself into a cosmos." His *What is Rhythm? An Essay* (in ten chapters and fifteen excursus) was published in 1925: one lays it down with a feeling that the complexities of his cosmos escape chaos by a hair's breadth only. Like Saintsbury he began with the Greek metrists, but unlike Saintsbury he became preoccupied with their theory of ratios and became not a 'foot-scanner' but a complete 'timer.' Rhythm, he says, is "a relation of successive events in time," or more precisely, "that property of a sequence of events in time which produces on the mind of the observer the impression of proportion between the durations of the several events or groups of events of which the sequence is composed" (pp. 15, 16). And *"time,* in the sense of the relative durations of events, is the fundamental feature of rhythm" (p. 17). Again: "What we measure is, strictly speaking, not time but events in time" (p. 17). What are these events? They are sounds or groups of sounds. They may be characterized by stress and pitch—for "change of pitch also [besides its function in melody] demarcates events in time"—but "rhythm is a feature of such sequences as are recognizably proportioned to one another in duration—and of these alone." To sum up:

Now it cannot be denied that intensity (force, stress) and pitch play an important rôle in some of the manifestations of rhythm. But to call stress, pitch, etc., *factors* of rhythm implies more than this: it implies that rhythm *consists* of these things—that they are *ingredients* of rhythm. Yet this proposition seems on close examination to be untenable. For all these ingredients save one may be removed from a rhythmical sequence without making it unrhythmical; whereas if proportion between durations of the successive sounds or groups of sounds be wholly removed from the sequence its rhythmical character disappears (pp. 30, 34).

If stress be removed, one may inquire, how are we to recognize the proportional parts? Answer: "All measurement, whether in time or in space, must be from a point to a point, but the points are not necessarily marked by an accent or stress of the voice" (p. 57 n. 1). How else are they marked in speech? Can such an important role be denied the rights of factor? (Or is this mere word-quibbling?)

Professor William Thomson may be called a modified timer. He recognizes the values of time, duration, tempo, and quantity (giving each its distinctive meaning) in rhythm and insists with great vigor and even acerbity that rhythm is "an indissoluble compound of accent (in the wide sense) and quantity. Only for purposes of abstract discussion can these two elements be separated" (p. 26). When he essays a definition, it is this: "The rhythm of any portion of speech is that property of it in virtue of which its movement is consciously apprehended and reproduced as a unity. Or, to make another attempt: The rhythm of a speech-phrase is that complex of properties in virtue of which its movement is apprehended as a unity susceptible of conscious reproduction" (p. 141). This may be helpful or not; it is certainly not forbidding. But there is a catch. He defines a speech-phrase as "a portion of speech recognized by the ear as an entity separate from other portions, yet capable of further analysis, *e.g.* a line of verse, or a continuous bit of prose such as 'He was, in fact, almost as powerless as the king.'" Now this bit of prose is one phrase but two logical groups, one

within the other. Is this distinction important? Yes, for
Thomson not only insists that "what fills the time spaces
lies outside the rhythm" (p. 31), but asserts later (p.
158): "We now know that none of them—neither logical
groups, nor those of grammatical analysis, nor sense-
groups, nor sound-groups—form any part of rhythm."

In this way we are left with a rhythm that consists of
empty durations (though they contain accents indissolubly
compounded with quantity) which we are to apprehend
and reproduce as unities. This is comprehensible to the
philosophic mind perhaps, but it seems to add perplexity
where there were already difficulties enough.

Our guides have led us deeper into the maze, and
there are more turnings ahead.

There is, for example, the agogic accent. This was
born of music but has been ascribed to speech also. Before
it received its new name (from Dr. Hugo Riemann, in
his *Dynamik und Agogik*, 1884), it was simply the practice of emphasizing a note by dotting it or holding it beyond its allotted time and was called 'dotted-note' rhythm.
From this Riemann advanced to a theory that music was
a series of crescendos and dimuendos (dynamic) of proportioned lengths (agogic). Hints of this idea have appeared in the preceding pages; and it is not unrelated
to Wundt's belief that the pleasure of rhythm comes from
a repetition of feelings of tension and the contrast between them and feelings of relaxation. In fact, Wundt's
view may be merely a psychological explanation of our
apprehension of all rhythm, with stress or strain (with
its accompanying relaxation) as the middle term. The
same idea has been pushed even further, to the exclusion
of time altogether: "If we take the ground that grouping
in rhythm is an affective experience and if we place it

simply in the dimension of strain and relaxation it at once becomes clear why no regular time relations are necessary. The regularity becomes a matter of recurrence of strain at the end of a definite cycle."[3] And this in turn may help to explain how we get our impression of equal or similar periods of time which by absolute measurement are not equal at all.

Thus the wheel comes full circle, and we go out where we came in. But, in any case, the circle revolves: for there is the rhythm of the flowing line, in which the groupings are so indistinct as to be vaguely felt rather than perceived. "Flowing line," says Miss Griffith, "rather than recurrent pattern is the characteristic of good fluid prose, a symphonic rather than an antiphonal rhythm" (pp. 57-58). "Flux and reflux, swell and cadence, that is the movement for a sentence," says DeQuincy, putting it all together.

And lastly, again: "Horwicz calls rhythm the only measure of time, and ventures the assertion that a being whose experience did not manifest periodicity could gain no conception of its nature. Time does not make rhythm, but rhythm time."[4] Take now two specimens for examination.

> A wild west Coast, a little Town,
> Where little Folk go up and down,
> Tides flow and winds blow:
> Night and Tempest and the Sea,
> Human Will and Human Fate:
> . . . .
> Let me sing of what I know.

"A wild west Coast" is metrically two iambs; so is "a little Town"; and so is "-est and the Sea"; but no mechanically measured time can make them equal to one another or equal to "Tides flow." It is the sort of 'time' created by the rhythm and the expectancy of equality which enables us to regard them as approximately equal, i.e., sufficiently equal, to satisfy the ear.

But take the description of Finn's favorite wolf-hound:

> Yellow feet had Bran, and red ears;
> She had a white spot on her breast;
> The rest of her body was black with this exception,
> She was sprinkled with white over the loins.

So printed, this looks like verse. But it will not scan in the ordinary way. It begins well enough, but the last two lines seem more like prose. Try it then as prose, and find perhaps (but that is another story) one of the mysteries of 'modern verse.' The first line has three stresses, not metrical stresses but centers of emphasis when spoken as prose: "Yellow feet . . . Bran . . . red ears." So the second line has three: "white" and "spot" and "breast." So the third line: "rest of her body . . . black . . . this exception." And so the fourth: "sprinkled . . . white . . . loins." Accordingly then, if you have the secret, you find four three-stress members of a prose sentence, which are 'equal' in the same sense as "A wild west Coast" and "Tides flow" are 'equal.' The rhythm, once you have found it out, has made the time.

This is a lesson of the first importance. The prosodist may agree with the poet in saying

> But at my back I always hear
> Time's winged chariot hurrying near.

But the theorist who insists on isochronous measures will have difficulty in making "Time's wing-" even approxi-

mately equal to "-ed char-." *Time* has betrayed him
flagrantly.

One who puts together all the above confusion, of
inconsistency and contradiction, of circles and epicycles,
may be reasonably accused of dulness—or malice. It was
Thomson himself who, among all his fulminations and
jeremiads at the nonbelievers, cheerfully admitted that
'rhythmology' "is already a terror to all but the voracious
for miscellaneous knowledge." Yet patience is reckoned
among the virtues, and the Old Testament worthies em-
brace Job with Jeremiah; and Ecclesiastes, along with
other comforting things, remarks: "All the rivers run into
the sea; yet the sea is not full."

So then, if time does not make rhythm but rhythm
time, there will be questions to raise about time. What
is 'time'?

vi

The timers start with time as a measure or means of
measurement. What right have they to do so? Surely it
would seem to be necessary to measure time before using
it for a measure of something else. This is an ancient
problem, complicated by misunderstandings and contra-
dictions. Can we have it both ways: time the measured
and the measurer? If not, which is first and fundamental?

Time can be measured only in terms of something
else, usually in terms of movement through space, and
most successfully nowadays by the pendulum. So we or-
dain an artificial time, derived from the movement of the
stars and reduced to instruments called clocks, and say
that this is the measure of rhythm. It may be highly convenient, but is it not also a circular argument? You may
reply that there is no need for *us* to involve ourselves in

the philosophical problems of the nature of Time; but it *is* of direct concern to us that we avoid the fallacy of using a word in different senses unawares.

Take now the neat summing up of a specialist:

For the psychologist, time is essentially the content of the inner sense of sequence and duration, while for the physicist it is the measurable time of the outer world of motion. . . . The metaphysical concept cannot be equated with either. . . . The metaphysical concept of Time is based on time as objectively given, for the metaphysician can never equate or confuse time with our awareness of it.

Or again:

Even the problem presented by the time-order of the perceptions alone is a difficult one. We constantly assume that at least we know definitely the order of the succession of our perceptions, whether or no these have any correspondence to the actual succession of external events of which they are perceptions. Our normal experience is one of succession of the before-and-after relation; we know that (in terms of perception) the mental event B follows the mental event A, both of them perceptions. We appear quite confident that we saw the flash of lightning and then we heard the thunder, that the first words of a spoken sentence were perceived by us and then subsequently the last. . . . But, unfortunately, while this confidence appears justified in practical affairs and in relation to matters not too distant in memory, it is found that if the perceptions be more intricate and more closely related by very small intervals our judgment *even of the order of our perceptions* becomes confused, erroneous, and uncertain, more especially if they involve events in different series or involve different senses. Sigwart brings this out quite clearly in his discussion of the 'Determination of Time'. Our inner life does not progress in a simple line of successive perceptions, for several distinguishable series proceed simultaneously. 'We do not cease to see while we hear, and hearing continues while we consciously endeavour to compare the seen and the heard.' (Gunn, p. 165)

Thus nothing is simple to the inquiring spirit, and we who are accustomed to take things as we find them, naïvely, are reminded that in the complex activities of comprehending at the same time the intellectual or emotional content, or both, of a piece of prose, and also giving heed to the succession of sounds as sounds as well as to their relations to the content of which they are symbols, may run grave risks of illusion and error. No steps can be made too easy for us, no hesitations may be allowed to become too disheartening, no doubts too deterrent. For language is certainly a series of events involving different senses, proceeding simultaneously. It is a continual miracle that we get on with it as well as we do. There should be no surprise that we misapprehend and miss as much as we do. The mystery is that we can make anything at all of the mystery. Then for our comfort be it said that where all is dark a little light is welcome. And what is a little error where nothing is clear?

But our Time Philosopher continues, after a few pages:

It is not difficult for Sigwart to show that Kant was unable to distinguish what occurs when we see a house and when we see a boat gliding down a river. It is quite absurd to say that the perception of the parts of a house is successive in the same sense as the perception of the positions of the moving boat. The succession involved is quite different in the two cases, and Kant seems to have got into the difficulty by his erroneous generalization that all perception of a manifold is successive. This is to confuse disastrously the perception of the co-existent parts of an object with the perception of successive events.

Thus in our perception of language, which is a succession of sounds in unmistakable temporal sequence like the changing positions of the boat, and is also, when read from the printed page, a succession of words whose parts are perceived as coexistent like the parts of a house, and a succession of syntactically, logically, organized parts which are themselves wholes, like parts of a larger house or a planned group of houses, we must distinguish between the succession of sounds as acoustic phenomena, which is certainly a matter of time, and the accumulating awareness of the symbolic significance of those sounds, which, though a series of parts, represent a whole of coexistent parts. In so far as rhythm is of time only, we can properly speak of the rhythm of language only with regard to its acoustic properties, and the meaning or content of language is excluded from the province of rhythm altogether—unless it is possible that both the sounds and their meanings can be brought into a single time sequence. How this is to be done is our next problem.

But first there is another corollary, perhaps useful, to be drawn from these general observations. The student of prose rhythm may dismiss the metaphysical concept of time as outside his bailiwick; he need not sign up with the idealists or realists, Platonists or Aristotelians, Bergsonians or Einsteinians. But he must recognize the distinction between the perceived time of the psychologist and the artificially measured time of the physicist—though Absolute Time in the Newtonian sense has been abandoned. This means that he must recognize the discrepancy between laboratory measurements, even those based on a large number of records by carefully selected readers, and the effects of sequence and duration pro-

duced on the inner sense of the common reader. If the
latter has this sense at all, or at all developed and trained,
he comes much closer to what we mean by prose rhythm
than any accumulation of mechanically based statistics can
possibly bring him. For it is psychological time that matters, and the best statistical accounts are but a poor relation. It is for this reason—our sense of time being weak
and our feeling for relative intensities being strong—
that we may regard stress and time, long hereditary enemies, as friendly brothers, as in fact Siamese twins, with
different heads and arms doing the same thing. To count
stresses is to measure time by the only method commonly
and reliably accessible to us.

Now to return to the question of bringing time and
meaning into a single sequence. Hints of this have appeared already. It is a problem which baffles the specialists, and therefore not much can be expected from a
layman.

If time flows, what does it flow *through?* Space?
What is space? If time is a stream, as the poets make out,
what are its banks? These questions are unsettling, perhaps unanswerable; but for the moment one approach to
the answers is the rejection of 'Empty Time' as unintelligible and concentration on the events. Time is a way of
measuring successive events, and if there were nothing
to measure, time would have no interest for us. All that
as rhythmologists we care about time is its function in
producing the effect of rhythm; and since rhythm is not
made out of nothing, that is, not made out of time without events, we cannot neglect the material for the method
of using it, and the material is not only the acoustic values
of language but the symbolic as well. Rhythm exists

therefore not merely in the sounds, what we hear, but in the meanings, what we understand. Or, to revert to the terminology used at the outset: conceptual rhythm is temporal, perceptual rhythm is both temporal and eventual. It includes what we accept or organize as temporal relations and what we apprehend or organize into temporal relations.

For the metaphysician this may be a specious oversimplification. For us it will have to do. If it seems to make the definition of rhythm too broad, we reply that we have no use for rhythm without such inclusiveness.

Thus I have put down here much else for which we may have no real use, but it seemed necessary to face and either surmount or circumvent the obstacles already in the path. To call them lions would add to the excitement but overrate their viciousness. They were obstacles, however.

The paradox may be exhibited in another form.

The psychologists are agreed—no, not quite that, for specialists are seldom in full agreement—that the awareness of duration turns, at least in part, on "(1) the number of events happening in the period and their pleasurability, interest, or monotony: (2) the concentration of our attention on time itself during the period; and (3) the unity or diversity of the matters involved." This applies to time in general and explains among other things why happiness is short and boredom is long; but it concerns us in so far as it emphasizes the contradiction between pleasure, say, the perusal of good prose, and the necessity of paying attention to the lapse of time in order to measure duration in order to appreciate the rhythm. That is, the more we enjoy a prose passage the less attention we give to the element of time during the perusal;

or, in other words, the sense of time is in abeyance during our enjoyment of rhythm. Or have we a delicate inner instrument of consciousness which measures for us while attention is abroad? There is no evidence of it except in the assumption of the 'timers.' (The psychologists are at variance on this point, and there are some uncanny evidences for it among the abnormal and the somnambulists.) But for most of us it is agreed that the measurement of duration, except within a very narrow range, is uncertain and faulty.

"Let us welcome the psychologist on our own ground," says one of the modern prosodists, "and keep on telling him how foolish he looks."

The contention that all rhythm is based upon time is so nearly self-evident as to be not a contention but an axiom. We all live and move and have our being in time; all our experience is a series of presents, a movement in time—including speech. Articulate speech and printed prose: a continuum of sounds and silences, a movement in time. We never escape from time; it is one of our dimensions.

The real question is then: What is the character of the successive events which gives us the sense of rhythm? The answer is: Our awareness either that a similar event has preceded the present one or our expectancy that a similar one is to follow. Perception of A, perception of B united with memory of A, perception of C united with . . . and so on.

The word *similar* has to be examined, for it has two meanings. It does not of course mean 'identical.'

But events both occur in time, that is, in the continuum, and also occupy time—unless they are mere in-

stants or abstractions. Thus the similar events are not only
in time but *of* time. Which has caused confusion in some
minds. For one characteristic is likeness in itself, and
another characteristic is likeness in duration; but in both
it is necessary to distinguish between similarity and identity. Successive events may be identical in themselves
and only similar in duration, or, the other way around,
identical in duration and only similar in themselves: the
old law of uniformity in variety, or variety in uniformity.

Music affords a good illustration. The intervals of
time between the bars are identical, or are assumed to be,
though actually they may differ considerably. But the
rhythm of music is not in the equality of the bars alone,
or even chiefly, but in the differences of their content and
in their grouping.

All this means only that rhythm is a series of units or
elements or groups which are similar not necessarily in
themselves or necessarily in their duration, but the more
alike they are in both characteristics the more obvious is
the rhythm, and the more unlike they are in one characteristic or the other, provided the impression of similarity is maintained or is induced, the more interesting
the rhythm is. Time in the sense of duration is only one
aspect of the similarity: and for the impression of similarity the idea of expectancy is paramount. For if the expectancy is strong enough we may readily assimilate or
organize into similarity things which are palpably unlike
either in themselves or in duration or even in both.

vii

In the activity of composing, that is, of using language
as a means of communication, the attention is distributed
over three operations: (1) the separation and organiza-

tion of the various parts of what it to be communicated, the ideas, thought, feeling, and so on; (2) the arrangement of these according to the forms of language, that is, to meet the requirements of standard syntax, usage, and all the other conveniences which make the meaning accessible to the reader or hearer; and (3) the artistic adjuncts which not only assist in giving force and clearness to the meaning but also make it agreeable and attractive. These three operations vary in emphasis and proportion according to the ideas and the purpose of communicating them; they exert, moreover, mutual influences, each one tending to determine or to alter the others; and not only do they run together in such quick succession as to seem simultaneous, but they are subject in revision to further alterations and adaptations in the interests of precision, satisfaction to the ear, and the final harmony—which all have their necessary appropriate functions.

Rhythm is busy in each of these operations—in making the ideas flow in natural and logical sequence, in accepting or molding the latent metrical movement of English words, and in the parallel expression of parallel ideas, and a fortiori in the cultivation for higher prose of sound effects and all that which both stimulates the imagination and delights the ear. Often the degree to which one or another prevails is an index of the kind and quality of the prose.

An ingenious view was put forward some years ago which even if not convincing is at least suggestive. "Any series of impressions or of nerve and muscle reactions will irresistibly take a rhythmic form, except when interfered with by the conscious effort that is involved in the process of indirect comprehension"; and thus "the irregularity of the rhythm of prose is due . . . to the mental process of reflective thought and of forming judgments."[5] With a little adjustment this can be made to fit the act of composition as well as that of apprehension. You note the assumption that spontaneous language is naturally and so to say irresistibly rhythmic; and to a certain degree this is true. The natural expression of intense feeling—poetry —is very likely to be rhythmic. But the conscious effort to get something said, clearly and intelligibly, that is, to communicate something which cannot be immediately apprehended—ideas and the complex relations of facts— is an interference with this natural rhythm. Similarly the required effort to grasp the meaning of language which communicates ideas and the complex relations of facts interferes with the perception of the rhythms which may exist, latent or not, in this language.

True. But what of the poet's effort in molding his natural or normal language to the requirements of meter, and of the reader's effort in absorbing the 'poetry' and at the same time recognizing the enhanced values which spring from the metrical forms? Here is interference on both levels, and yet the rhythm is more complicated in that it is the resultant of prose rhythms *and* metrical patterns, and more powerful in that it calls for greater effort on the part of writer and reader and hence greater satisfaction when the effort is successful.

Or is this just another paradox?

ix

The theoretical regularity of equal measures in music, even when the executants are highly skilled, shows considerable variation. This we knew, and it has been proved by laboratory experiment. The variation is partly unconscious, owing to the unreliability of our motor reactions, and differs greatly among individuals. But it may also be intentional, for much of the power of musical rhythm is due to a subtle deliberate avoidance of mechanical regularity. The musicians often call it phrasing.

Even more variation from the metronomical regularity is to be expected in verse; for in verse there is no theoretical bar measurement and no assumption of isochronism. (There are two exceptions to this statement, one for a certain kind of popular, fundamentally temporal verse, and one for a certain kind of reader; but the admission does not invalidate the generalization.) Such time values as there are seem to derive from conventions and from personal habits in pronouncing the words (the acoustic values), modified by the demands of expression (the communication values), both adjusted by an easy give-and-take to the metrical schema, which is based on theoretical equivalence of the bars or feet.

In prose, where this last, the formal metrical pattern, is absent, there are only the acoustic and expressional values. The rhythm derives from them alone, and its patterns (if they may be called such) are therefore free from the demands of theoretical equality of measure. Certain rhetorical or syntactic arrangements may take the place of metrical feet and form a kind of extended meter —as Yeats said of "the antithetical prose of the seventeenth century, which is itself a true metre." But though the rhythmic principle of repeated equal or similar units is not to be denied, the prose units cannot be held to equality in the same strictness.

x

Slow rhythms are the hardest to apprehend because

the memory of successive units, or rather, of anterior units in relation to those which have followed, is not sufficiently strong. Rapid ones, jingling tunes, are easiest. But between the latter, which quickly satiate by their monotony, and the former, from the effort needed to cope with them, there is the usual middle ground broad enough to contain all that we need for artistic pleasure.

In long poems the formal meter is an aid and support to memory and a help to overcome the handicap of flagging memory. The meter is itself a metronome calling and re-calling attention to a schematic pattern. But in prose relatively short rhythmic stretches have to suffice: we have not ordinarily enough energy to spare from the content to give to long sustained movements. Hence the prose writer's problem is to supply an artificial framework which is at the same time easily referable to his matter and perceptible to his reader. A history of prose rhythm would be an account of the various methods of meeting this problem. The two easy solutions are: (1) reliance on parallel structure and obvious balance, and (2) metrical inlays. And both of these the judicious reader soon wearies of. Failing these, the judicious writer turns to long swelling undulations, the involutions of compound-complex sentences (a partial disguise of parallel constructions)—the manner of Donne and of the later seventeenth century, of Macaulay and of Ruskin in his Hookerish periods. The principle is still the same, however, but its obviousness is reduced by increase in dimension; attention is distracted from the plainness of the pattern; and a veil is drawn across the machinery, so that the effect is felt without being clearly seen. At any rate, this is how it should be, and perhaps as it was intended to be. But success grows by what it feeds on; confidence

begets pride and pride *hybris*. The pendulum swings in-
eluctably, and great achievements of rhythm lie between
the wide arcs.

xi

As part of the aesthetic pleasure which one derives
from poetry is due to the versification, that is, to the
special way in which the language is molded to the metrical forms, so there is an analogous aesthetic pleasure de-
rivable from prose, but this is more difficult to recognize
and explain because in prose there is no norm like the
patterns of meter from which the arrangements of a prose
sentence vary and to which they return. To watch the
slight novelty, the continual divergences between the
natural reading of a sentence and the reading of it as part
of a metrical plan is one of the simple pleasures of
poetry; and this is absent from prose simply because the
natural reading is the only one and whatever rhythm
prose may have must inhere in this natural reading. The
requirements of grammar and the conventions of word-
order are the best that prose has to serve as a 'norm'
corresponding to meter in verse. Prose must therefore
get its rhythmic effects by a special heightening of its
own ways and means, a continual concealed borrowing
from outside.

"The rule of scansion in verse," said Stevenson, "is to
suggest no measure but the one in hand; in prose to suggest no measure at all. Prose must be rhythmical, and
it may be as much so as you will; but it must not be
metrical. It may be anything, but it must not be verse. A
single heroic line may very well pass and not disturb
the larger stride of the prose style; but one following
another will produce an instant impression of poverty,
flatness, and disenchantment."

"The very freedom of prose, its want of conventions, of settled prosody, of musical inspiration, give wider scope for failure and afford no beaten paths. . . . Prose puts forth its lonely skiff upon a boundless sea."—Frederic Harrison.

". . . the total irregularity of prose."—Herbert Spencer.

Prose has a freer and higher music than verse—"pure musique et presque céleste . . . qui ne caresse un instant l'oreille que pour lui échapper aussitôt."—Henri Bremond.

"And of course there is a great deal of prose which, consciously or unconsciously, adopts the poetic method. The background of metrical sameness is not quite so regular [not quite!]; on the other hand, the possibilities of rhythmical variation are not so great, simply because the sameness is deficient. Hence arise the peculiar dangers of poetic prose [metrical prose]; in which it is much more difficult than in poetry to make the rhythmical variations really perceptible."—J. M. Murry.

I think there is a fallacy here besides the confusion of 'poetic' and 'metrical.' Others have been similarly puzzled. Compare Stevenson, telling us that prose is harder to write than verse, "for in prose the pattern itself has to be invented, and the difficulties first created before they can be solved."

"The prose of Chateaubriand makes us think of beautiful verse, the verse of Racine makes us think of beautiful prose."—Henri Bremond.

"Verse is written in lines with a certain number of metrical feet each; prose is written in paragraphs and has

what we call rhythm."—Edmund Wilson. Could anything be simpler?

"The poet's Muse is like a mistress, whom we keep
only while she is young and beautiful, durante bene
placito; the Muse of prose is like a wife, whom we take
during life, *for better for worse*."—Hazlitt.

As in any prose the flowers should not be conspicuous,
so in rhythmical prose the music should be *over*heard and
not a distraction.

"At all events, I am nearly certain that whatever rich
and pure purples are introduced locally, by the great
colourists, nothing is so destructive of all fine colour as the
slightest tendency to purple in the general tone."—*Modern Painters*.
This from Ruskin!

While most of us, standing on the solid ground of
tradition and authority, would maintain that verse is not
only the proper form of poetry but the finest form for
saying great things, there may be a few, and Landor
among them—"Poetry was always my amusement; prose
my study and business"—who would hold that prose, with
its "infinite variety," freed from the formalities of rime
and meter, possesses all the possible means of rhythmic
effect and power except one (and that one, regularity,
verse is always attempting to escape from); that prose is
the superior medium, the best prose, of course subtly
managed but not overmannered. What is there aside
from pure song which prose cannot do so well as verse—
if we were not already prejudiced? And why, except in
pure song, does verse always try to become prose, or to
come as close as it dares?

But the answer must be, against Landor, that while prose has everything but regularity, verse has everything including regularity. And so the greater includes the lesser, as it should. The answer in another form, moreover, is that nearly everyone, even after confessing to all ancient prejudices, feels and admits feeling that showpieces of prose are suspect, both for their illicit origin—a shadow of illegitimacy if not of incest—and for their air of affectation. Verse is frankly artificial and enjoys the rights and perquisites of artificiality. But prose aiming at the effects of verse is a plain man in masquerade.

Still, as Sir Roger would put it, there is much to be said on both sides.

"An orderly and sweet sentence, by gaining our ear, conciliates our affections."—Chatham to Chesterfield, in Landor's *Imaginary Conversations*.

"Il n'y a pas de prose."—Mallarmé.

xii

"Now Plato in many passages owes his elegance directly to the rhythm, which is, so to speak, long drawn out, and without basement or amplitude, of which the former suits the plain and forcible, the latter the elevated style. His members seem to glide along and to be neither altogether metrical nor unmetrical, as in . . . 'in warbling and revelling he passes his life wholly.' And once more: 'should he see any sympton of passion, like steel would he temper it.' Thus framed the sentences are manifestly elegant and harmonious. But if you invert the order and say 'he would temper it like steel' or 'he passes all his life,' you will rob the language of its charm, which resides wholly in the rhythm. Certainly it is not

to be found in the thought, nor in the choice of words."
—Demetrius, *On Style* (trans. W. Rhys Roberts).

In prose as in verse—in every attempt to realize the
full possibilities of language—there are to be distinguished both the relation of the sounds as symbols and the
relation of the sounds in themselves. The one is commonly recognized though often neglected in practice; the
other is often overlooked or despised. It is a characteristic of the Greek rhetoricians that they were interested in
the sounds of language—the sounds of spoken language
—for both poetry and prose were composed to be heard,
and they chose their examples from Homer and Plato
without discrimination. They assumed that prose was as
much an art as verse. They were generally not concerned with pragmatic prose: the elements of clarity and
force they took for granted and concentrated their interest
on the finesses of style. For they knew that Plato and
Demosthenes had done so.

We have much to learn from the Greek rhetoricians,
but because of the differences between their language and
ours, between Greek and English, their analyses of prose
rhythm are not helpful. They began with the *letters*,
confusing these with the sounds of which they are merely
the symbols; and they associated, even as some modern
poets have done, certain magic qualities with each. Thus
Dionysius of Halicarnassus tells us that "λ falls pleasur-
ably on [the sense of hearing], and is the sweetest of the
semi-vowels; while ρ has a rough quality, and is the noblest of its class . . . σ is an unattractive, disagreeable
letter." Similarly with syllables. Dionysius then proceeds to the feet, which are of course quantitative in a
sense quite other than English feet, and describes them

in language suggestive of the language of fortunetellers. The pyrrhic is "neither impressive nor solemn," the spondee "possesses great dignity and much stateliness," the iamb is "not ignoble," the trochee is "less manly . . . and more ignoble." Then he runs through the trisyllabic feet. The tribrach is "mean and wanting in dignity and nobility and nothing noble can be made out of it," whereas the molossus is "elevated and dignified, and has a mighty stride"; the amphibrach is "enervated" and "feminine"; the anapest "possesses much dignity"; the dactyl is "decidedly impressive"; and so on. He then illustrates these observations by analyses of passages from Thucidydes, Plato, and Demosthenes.

This may sound like hocus-pocus, but Dionysius is very serious, and what is more, his method has been adopted and pursued by some of the most distinguished modern English analysts. So Saintsbury writes, on page 316: "the procession in bulk of 'heraldries' and 'hieroglyphics'—the dactyl to the dochmiac—and the simple trochee 'darkness' to the pæon plus anapest of 'on the tablets of the brain' . . ." And in his Appendix III his Axiom 1 reads: "The Rhythm of Prose like the Metre of Verse can, in English as well as in the classical languages, be best expressed by applying the foot-system, or system of mathematical combination of 'long' and 'short' syllables." Most of the forty-odd inferences and suggestions which follow are but developments of this position. Thus a marking of foot-scansion, a little abracadabra of metaphor, a lively epithet, and the trick is done. For example: "in English, where the trochee is the acorn-drop (in fall and rebound) from our ancestral oaks, and the trickle of the water-spring from the rock whence we were born" (p. 7 n. 1). Saintsbury has many fine qualities

and his book on prose rhythm is indispensable, but one
may say without straining that his principles were wrong
and his method false. His ear was good, however, and
his taste generally sound. It is something, surely, to have
written an excellent book of 480 pages, an anthology of
the best specimens, often with brilliant commentary, but
it is a splendid superstructure on hollow foundations.

Not that Saintsbury made the mistake of borrowing
his doctrine merely from Dionysius or "the three greatest" of the Greek rhetoricians (Demetrius, Dionysius,
and 'Longinus'), who themselves expanded and developed Aristotle, as one would expect; but that he permitted himself the false assumption that English syllables
are determinably long and short and can be treated quan-
titatively as in Greek and Latin prosody, and went on
from there applying the Greek method. Rhythm in the
light of modern definition was foreign to his ideas; isochronism did not interest him. He took, however, a simple
delight in the "pæon *plus* anapest" and like "the Hali-
carnassian" found a mystical beauty in certain of the
ancient feet.

So much and no more on Saintsbury. With all his
shortcomings he cut a wide swath, and we all follow in
his path, more or less.

xiii

It is possible that the motor processes of reading, particularly the backward and forward movement of the
eye, not only in crossing the page back and forth regularly, but also in certain 'regressions' to pick up the syntactic patterns, with the attendant pauses, may have some
obscure influence in setting up a feeling of rhythm. This
would be more likely in reading verse, but might also
operate in reading prose.

xiv

For most of us it is difficult to distinguish, except abstractly, the sounds of language from their semantic values, since by definition words do not exist without meaning. That is, sound and sense are inseparable. In discussing prose rhythm it may be permissible to think of the sounds as the melody of language and the meanings as harmony. But this is a convenience of expression and should not be abused.

Just as in music the trained ear does not easily follow all the intricacies of the pattern without reference to the musical text, and the untrained ear cannot achieve more than a vague outline of sound, pleasing or unpleasing, just so the reader of prose without special preparation is obliged, and often content, to be satisfied with only a general notion of the effects, simple and cumulative, which the sounds of language produce. He is negligent of what he misses and even sometimes resentful of any effort to draw it to his attention. He trusts his ear.

But when a passage is read by different speakers the variations both in detail and in the large are such that we are driven to assume a sort of ideal rendering, which is purely imaginary and which differs not only from your way and mine of reading the passage, but also from your and my notions of the way we read it. What you and I hear when we read silently or only partially vocalize, what you hear and what I hear when you read aloud or when I read aloud, are six quite different series of sounds, and the ideal reading is a seventh.

xv

Pitch—the word is used in two senses which should be distinguished: (1) the musical tone of notes in one of the standard scales, based on the rate of vibration; and (2) the rise and fall of the voice in speaking, variations in tone which generally do not conform to the musical scales. It is in the latter sense, much the same as inflection or intonation, that we use the word in discussing rhythm. This sense corresponds more nearly to melody and phrasing in music than the other—absolute pitch. Melody has its curves and contours, its phrases and 'sentences,' which may be called groups of variations in pitch.

A simple method of estimating the role of pitch in rhythm is to whisper a sentence. Obviously something is not there, but the rhythm is. Basta? Basta.

xvi

It cannot be too often or emphatically repeated that language is both a series of sounds as sounds and a series of sounds as symbols of what we call meaning. This includes both words and signals. It is a kind of un-noted music with its own system of changing pitch and intensity, duration and pause. No adequate way of representing this 'orchestration' has yet been devised.

The flow of musical sounds is difficult enough to represent and interpret; but the flow of language sounds is still more difficult because it combines two such different elements: it engages not only the attention of the ear and that part of the mind which apprehends and distinguishes the variations of sound and silence, but also the attention of the mind as it receives the logical and the emotional content of the words.

All the qualities of sound work together, closely related and interdependent—some more powerful than others, now in one place, now in another—and it is usually a hopeless undertaking to dissociate them. Sometimes we want to stand off and admire the richness of the fabric. At other times we want to turn it over and study the manner of its weaving.

The advantage of stress for analysis is that it is nearly always conscious to the speaker and unmistakable. There are many degrees of it, but the main accent of a word is pretty well fixed. In phrase, clause, and sentence the word accent may be subordinated to rhetorical considerations; it is subordinated and sometimes obscured; but it is there as a guide and is never entirely lost. It is, when all is said, the backbone of speech rhythm. Considerations of time, of length of syllable, are ever present and ever active, but time cannot be, in the nature of the English language, so consciously a determinant as stress. There can be no rhythm without it because it is inherent in the principle of rhythm and it is inherent in language. The same is true of pitch. Like the members of the Athanasian trinity, time, stress, and pitch are coequal; yet one is *primus inter pares* and that is—for the purposes of analyzing prose rhythm—stress.

II

Rhythm as Sound

i

LANGUAGE COMES TO US in two forms: aural, through the ear, and visual, through the eye. In the one form it is a series of sounds which are symbols of various meanings. In the other, it is a series of letters which are symbols of sounds which are themselves symbols of meanings.

All language is therefore a union of sounds and meanings, and the rhythms of language will presumably include both these properties. The study of rhythm must take account of both. In more or less obscure ways each may influence the other.

When these properties of language are closely examined they appear to be of no little complexity. A whole volume has been written on *The Meaning of Meaning*, without solving all the riddles. Phoneticians, the specialists of speech-sounds, have long been occupied with analysis of their problems, also without solving them all. It is enough, now, to recognize some of these difficulties without attempting to wrestle with them at length; only so much as may be helpful in clarifying the questions of language rhythm need be undertaken.

ii

The smallest unit of spoken language is the phoneme, the simplest isolable sound, which, in combination with other phonemes, comprises our syllables and words. After these come the phrase group, the clause, the sentence, and the paragraph. All of these share, in different ways, the four properties of sound: duration, intensity, pitch, and tone-quality ('timbre').[1]

Duration is the relative length of time occupied in the utterance of a syllable or group of syllables;[2] and in so far as time is an essential element of rhythm duration is of the first importance. It is also of the greatest difficulty. Laboratory instruments can record with accuracy the elapsed time of spoken syllables and words, but unfortunately the ear and brain have no comparable equipment, and our individual sense of time, which is what we nearly always depend upon, is as variable and untrustworthy as that of taste or color. Sometimes, with unwarrantable confidence, prosodists and others have attempted to formulate rules for determining the length of English syllables; but the syllables still refuse to be so cabined, cribbed, and confined. In classical prosody certain conventions obtained (that is, were accepted by the poets), though the critics recognized that some long syllables were longer than other long syllables and that the ratio of one long to two shorts was not always constant. No such conventions, however, obtain in English, either for the poets or for readers of prose. Mason, in the eighteenth century, lightly assumed that all accented syllables are long and all unaccented syllables short—which is as reasonable as to say that all tall men are lean and all short men are fat. Saintsbury and Dr. Bridges do not seem to have got much further. It is true, no doubt, that certain vowels and consonants and certain combinations of them tend to be longer than others; thus *chasm* occupies more time in normal utterance than *cam*, *knight* than *knit*, *shoal* than *boat*, *heart* than *hat*, *sea* at the end of a sentence than in *seacoast*, and so on.[3] But observe what happens to the length of *red* in these lines:

And the sea-folk labour and the red sails lift,
They rush in red and purple from the red clouds of the morn.

And what the poet does for metrical effect the reader of prose can do and does habitually do for rhetorical or emotional reasons. Note the different lengths of 'how' in

♪ Hów did you | knów?
♪ How d'you | dó?
♩ Hów? | you ásk.
♩. Hów | whén | whý did it | háppen?[4]

Or compare "He maketh me to lie down in green pastures" in the familiar singsong (emphasis of "mak-," "down," "pas-") with the same sentence as it should be spoken with proper attention to "lie" and "green." Whatever the other differences, it is plain that the relative lengths of syllables differ in the two readings. A further example may be seen in three readings of part of the famous sentence in Pater's description of La Gioconda. One of these shows the exact durations recorded by laboratory instruments (which let us call A^5); the second is Professor Thomson's analysis of his own delivery (which let us call B^6); and the third, which I add without comment, is Patterson's version tapped out as a series of drumbeats.[7]

"It is	the	land-scape		not	of		dreams
.5 1.15	.65	2.4	2.08 (.51)	1.25	.9		3.9 (.8)
¾ ¾	¾ |	1½	1½ 1½ |	1	1 |		1½

or	of		fan-	cy		but	of	plac	es"
.7	.82		1.4	1.85	(1.35)	.45	.8	1.4	1
¾	¾	|	1	1		¾	¾	|	1	1

B takes "It" and "is" as equal; A makes "is" more than twice as long as "It." B takes "not" and "of" as equal; A makes "not" nearly twice as long as "of." B takes "or" and "of" as each half as long as "dreams"; A (disregarding the pause[8]) makes "dreams" five times as long as "or" and "of," and more than two and a half times as long as the two together. B takes the two syllables of "fancy" as equal; A makes the second syllable appreciably (nearly one-fifth) longer. The similarities are likewise noticeable, but they only serve to emphasize the disparities.[9]

These illustrations will do to indicate the variability of syllabic length. They show also the unreliability of one's estimate of duration as compared with mechanical measurements; in other words, they show the difference between psychological time and real time. Equally uncertain, although less important in considerations of prose rhythm, is the time sense in pauses. Not all pauses are immediately related to rhythm—and in this of course language differs from music—and many are indistinguishable from sound-length. We pause, for example, at the end of a sentence, but we also 'hold' the final word or syllable; thus pause and silence are not synonymous. Again, we pause to give certain consonantal clusters distinct articulation—as in "the blithe crisp sentence"—without being aware of it or without giving the listener a sense of having paused. We usually pause over marks of punctuation, but not always, and we often pause when no such marks exist.[10] Though the habits of the reader and the nature of the subject matter play a large part in determining pauses, it seems that the more definitely rhythmical a passage the greater the number and the length of the pauses. The chief significance of pause, however, is in setting off groups or units of rhythm, and these pauses are in turn largely determined by the grammatical structure of the sentences. The two are obviously interdependent, but the nature of the relationship varies.

iii

Few readers are fully conscious of the measurement of time as they read or of the relative duration of the sounds, but all are aware of the relative energy with which certain syllables are spoken.[11] This relative energy takes two forms: the conventional accentuation of polysyllables (lexical accent) and the rhetorical emphasis with which certain words or syllables are uttered in order to bring out or strengthen their meaning. The phonetic term is 'intensity'; the common word is 'loudness'; a convenient term to include both senses is 'stress.'[12] This comparative stress is of the greatest importance in temporal rhythm; for since all measurement must be from one recognized point to another,[13] stress is not only the most convenient, but almost the only 'point' for measurement. So Mr. Classe puts it plainly: "The phenomenon which, by recurring at more or less regular intervals, creates what may be called, for want of a better phrase, a feeling of rhythm in speech, is generally admitted to be stress" (p. 12).

Word stress frequently coincides with length, and it is a fact that "the apparent loudness of a sound increases with the increase in duration, the objective intensity remaining constant."[14] But in speech sounds because of their other properties this is not always the fact, and it is never to be taken as a rule. In the recorded readings of the passage from Pater, above, the unaccented syllable of "landscape" is almost as long as the accented syllable; that of "fancy" actually longer. For some readers the last syllable of "goddesses," of "beautiful," and of "antiquity" (in note 8 above) was as long as, or longer than, the accented syllable. Yet most readers probably believe, until they can be convinced of their error, that they prolong the accented syllables and shorten the unaccented; and this belief must certainly affect the subjective rhythm.

One of the distinguishing marks of prose, in contrast to verse, is the function of rhetorical stress. In verse the latent or potential stresses are usually recognized for metrical purposes; in prose they are usually subordinated. (The very real and important effects of prose rhythm in verse are of course another matter.) This means that in prose not all the possible stresses are rhythm stresses, but only those 'landmarks' which require full emphasis to carry or reveal the burden of the sentence. This is especially evident in stage delivery, where the actor, not trying to make every word count, is obliged to 'get over' the most significant words only; and it is, incidentally, one of the actor's handicaps in speaking metrical lines. The words *peartree* and *appletree*, however they may differ acoustically, have each one prose stress. So from the point of view of rhythm there is a close relation between *every word count* and *each word count;* that is, the stress seems to be on the word *(each, every)* not on the syllable. And not only in *life insurance, all-expectant,* and similar long compounds do we feel a single rhythmic stress, but even two separate words may fuse into a single stress, as in Blake's "*No bird* soars *too high*, if he soars with his *own wings.*" Or consider this passage from Ruskin, in which I have italicized the rhythmic stress compounds: sometimes the chief emphasis is on one or another of the individual words and sometimes it is divided between them. In this form it may be called 'distributed stress.'

Twenty *years ago,* there was *no lovelier* piece of lowland scenery in *South England,* nor any *more pathetic* in the world, by its expression of sweet human character and life, than *that immediately* bordering on the sources of the Wandle, and including the *lower moors* of Addington, and the villages of Beddington and Carshalton, with all their pools and streams. *No clearer* or diviner waters *ever sang* with constant lips of the hand which "*giveth rain* from heaven;" *no pastures* ever lightened in *spring time* with *more passionate* blossoming; *no sweeter* homes ever hallowed the heart of the *passer-by* with their pride of peaceful gladness—*fain-hidden*—yet *full confessed.* The place remains, or, until a *few months ago,* remained, nearly unchanged in its larger features; but, with deliberate mind I say, that I have *never seen* anything so ghastly in its *inner meaning,*—not in Pisan Maremma,—not by Campagna tomb, —not by the *sand-isles* of the Torcellan shore,—as the slow stealing of aspects of reckless, indolent, animal neglect, over the delicate sweetness of that English scene: nor is *any blasphemy* or impiety—*any frantic* saying or godless thought —*more appalling* to me, using the best power of judgment I have to discern its sense and scope, than the insolent defilings of *those springs* by the *human herds* that drink of them. —*The Crown of Wild Olive,* Introduction.

iv

Each of our vowels has when whispered, that is, when produced without using the vocal cords, its own pitch or position in the musical scale. When voiced, as they are in normal speech, the vowels may be sounded at various pitches, though some are relatively lower and some relatively higher than others. In the main our consonants take their pitch from the vowels they are associated with, though they too have certain pitch characteristics, as for example the phoneme *k*, which is higher in *keel* than in *cool*. Thus, any series of syllables is a series of changing levels of pitch; and this is true not only of nonsense-syllables but a fortiori true in sentences spoken with inflections of the voice to express emotion.[15]

The significance of this pitch in the rhythm of English sentences is much disputed.[16] Most theorists make at least a grudging allowance for it, and some have even regarded it as a predominant factor. Certainly, with the rise and fall in the ever-varying inflections of the voice in reading or speaking there are frequent melodic waves which, when recognizable as recurrent units, produce a distinct rhythmic effect. They are probably more pervasive than is commonly admitted—they are of course obvious in singsong delivery—and are one of the prevailing characteristics of the 'flowing line' rhythm. But they are the most difficult of all forms to describe and analyze. At present we have too little accurate knowledge to justify any safe conclusions, and all I shall try to do here is to point a direction.[17]

In such a sentence as "When he narrated | the scene was before you," the rise and fall of the voice is plain enough; and likewise in "He expresses what all feel | but cannot say," where there is a kind of double apex before the pause.[18] And when these or similar curves are repeated successively, there is obvious rhythm: the upward glide, the returning fall, the upward glide again, and the corresponding fall. A single arc is but a rhythmic unit;

it is the succession of such waves that can be properly
called rhythm.

The same is true of longer sentences.

a   He brought himself into so composed a gravity,
b   that I never saw him laugh
c   and but seldom smile.

Here the curve is a simple a ^{b} c. Or take Goldsmith's

a   While his youth countenances the levity of his conduct
b   he may thus earn a precarious existence,
c   but when age comes on,
d   the gravity of which is incompatible with buffoonery,
e   then will he find himself forsaken by all
f   condemned in the decline of life to hang upon some rich
        family whom he once despised,
g   there to undergo all the ingenuity of studied contempt,
h   to be employed only as a spy upon the servants,
i   or a bugbear to frighten children into duty.

The curve is again a gradual rise and a gradual descent:

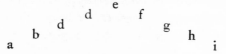

The following sentence, from Hallam's *Constitutional
History*, is more complex:

a   By this device,
b   which is as ancient as the reign of Henry II,
c   the fundamental privilege of trial by jury,
d   and the convenience of private suitors,
e   as well as accused persons,
f   was made consistent with a uniform jurisprudence;
g   and though the reference of every legal question,
h   however insignificant,
i   to the courts above must have been inconvenient in a still
        greater degree than at present,

j   it had doubtless a powerful tendency to knit together the
       different parts of England,

k   to check the influence of feudality and clanship,

l   to make the inhabitants of distant counties better acquainted
       with the capital city

m   and more accustomed to the course of government,

n   and to impair the spirit of provincial patriotism and animosity.

Here there is not so much the long rise and descent of
the whole, as within it the secondary rising and falling
curves, which may be represented something like this:

$$a \ _b \ c \ ^d \ e \ ^f \ g \ _h \ ^i \ _j \ k \ ^l \ _m \ n$$

Let these illustrations stand for our recognition of the
role of pitch or voice-inflection in English rhythm. It is
inalienable from our speech: a continual rising and falling, modified by subordinate curves and double or con-
trasted curves (known to the specialist as 'cymes') a continual undulation following the hesitancies and qualifications, the substitutions and retrogressions and reversals
of subtle and intricate syntactical arrangements. They are
plain to the listening ear but resistant to analytical
exposition.

But there is one word more. Take the word *æsthete*.
The accent is of course on the first syllable, but the long
vowel of the second not only makes the word, speaking
temporally, spondaic, but seems also to produce the effect
of a second accent. (This is rather different from the
simple compounds *peartree, boardwalk, armchair,* and so
on.) In certain American dialects this pitch-accent has become actually confused with stress-accent, as in the pro-
nunciation of *idea* with apparently strongest stress on the
first syllable. And in acoustical experiments it has been
found that among the lower tones intensity of stimulus

tends to lower the pitch (that is, the subjective judgment
of tone), and among the higher frequencies, when the
intensity is increased the pitch is raised.[19] So with records
of Mr. Martinelli's voice it appeared that "his pitch-in-
tensity curve showed a generally uniform increase of intensity with pitch.[20] Moreover, Professor Thomson, without the use of laboratory instruments, noted "the sym-
pathetic tendency to raise the pitch with the rise in intensity" (p. 99); and in another place seemed to admit
a kind of pitch which gives the illusion of stress.

From these slight evidences and helps it would not be
unfair to assume, tentatively, that pitch and stress go hand
in hand; they are likely to vary in direct ratio; and it may
be only a matter of opinion as to which is prepotent. One
writer indeed regards it as "demonstrated" that "wherever stress has an important function it is invariably accompanied by a change of tune, and . . . the change of
tune is really the part which matters, not the increase of
breathforce."[21] Perhaps true; yet as a concession to weakness we may be permitted to persist in confusing stress
with pitch, because they are so closely related, though
they are so different in origin, or rather in seeming to
neglect the one because we have no adequate way of deal-
ing with it as a factor of rhythm, and to concentrate on the
other as more readily and usefully manageable.[22]

v

The fourth property of sound, tone-quality or 'timbre,'
is sometimes included among the elements of rhythm;
but important as it may be for the æsthetic effects of
language, to reflect and intensify the emotional qualities
of words, it cannot really be said to share in the creation
of rhythm. It may enhance the effects produced by
rhythm; it cannot create them.

vi

Each bit of prose, whether spoken or read, is delivered
at a certain pace, which in music is called tempo. Tempo
or pace is not a factor of rhythm but a regulator of it.
It is also a revealer. It is determined almost wholly by
the subject matter—a solemn passage: *largo;* a lively one:
allegro. And the slower the tempo, the more marked are
the pauses, the holds, and the silences; and accordingly
the units become more distinct, the latent rhythms more
noticeable. By the same token an increased tempo tends
to level down the stresses, to hurry over the unstressed
elements, and so, increasing the distance between pauses,
diminish the marks by which the rhythmic groups are
signaled.

For a plain pedagogic illustration take the sentence
of Burke's from the *Letter to a Noble Lord,* which Mr.
Tempest quotes and marks with his reading (pp. 118-
19):

Had it pleased | God | to continue | to me | the hopes | of
succession, | I should have been, | according | to my medi-
ocrity, and the mediocrity | of the age | I live in, | a
sort | of founder of a family: | I should have left | a
son, | who, | in all | the points | in which | personal | merit |
can be viewed, | in science, | in erudition, | in genius, | in taste, |
in honour, | in generosity, | in humanity, | in every | liberal |
sentiment, | and every | liberal | accomplishment, | would
not | have shown himself | inferior | to the Duke | of Bed-
ford, | or to any | of those | whom he traces | in his line.

This scanning into feet after Saintsbury's manner gives
the appearance of longer pauses and slower movement
than I suppose Mr. Tempest had in mind. But waiving
that difference and using the bar to indicate chief pauses

and the accent to indicate emphases, one would read this
sentence today somewhat as follows:

Had it plèased Gòd to contínue to me | the hópes of
succéssion, | I should have bèen, according to my mediócrity, |
and the mediócrity of the àge I líve in, | a sort of fóunder
of a fámily: | and I should have left a sòn, whò, | in áll the
póints in which pérsonal mérit can be víewed,—etc.

This reading reduces not only the number of pauses and
the number of stresses but also reduces the relative quantity of stress at nearly all points; and the difference between the two readings is not a question of style but of
tempo alone. Further examples are hardly needed, but
here are two at least, written at almost the same time,
one *allegretto*, the other *andante ma non troppo*.

To begin, then, with Shakespeare. He was the man who of
all modern, and perhaps ancient poets, had the largest and
most comprehensive soul. All the images of nature were still
present to him, and he drew them, not laboriously, but
luckily; when he describes anything you more than see it,
you feel it too. Those who accuse him to have wanted learning give him the greater commendation: he was naturally
learned; he needed not the spectacles of books to read nature; he looked inwards, and found her there. I cannot say
he is everywhere alike; were he so, I should do him injury
to compare him with the greatest of mankind. He is many
times flat, insipid; his comic wit degenerating into clenches,
his serious swelling into bombast. But he is always great
when some great occasion is presented to him; no man can
say he ever had a fit subject for his wit and did not then raise
himself as high above the rest of poets,

Quantum lenta solent inter viburna cupressi.

The affairs of this world are like a curious but intricately
contrived comedy; and we cannot judge of the tendency
of what is past, or acting at present, before the entrance of

the last act, which shall bring in Righteousness in triumph; who, though she hath abided many a brunt, and has been very cruelly and despitefully used hitherto in the world, yet at last, according to our desires, we shall see the Knight overcome the Giant. For what is the reason we are so much pleased with the reading romances and the fictions of the poets, but that here, as Aristotle says, things are set down as they should be; but in the true history hitherto of the world, things are recorded indeed as they are, but it is but a testimony that they have not been as they should be. Wherefore, in the upshot of all, when we shall see that come to pass that so mightily pleases us in the reading the most ingenious plays and heroic poems, that long afflicted Virtue comes to the crown, the mouth of all unbelievers must be for ever stopped.

The first is from Dryden, of course; the second from the *Divine Dialogues* of More—Henry More.

III

Rhythm as Syntax—Balance—The Paragraph

i

THERE IS A SIMPLE repetition in Poor Richard's "God helps them that help themselves," in Thomas Paine's "These are the times that try men's souls," and in St. Paul's (*an.* 1611) "Whatsoever a man soweth, that shall he also reap." These are rhythms, if they are properly to be called such, of sound not of syntax. Yet if to the second we improvise a companion sentence: "These are the days that build character," and if we add the rest of what Paul wrote to the Galatians (7: 7, 8)—

Be not deceived: God is not mocked: for whatsoever a man soweth, that shall he also reap. For he that soweth to his flesh shall of the flesh reap corruption; but he that soweth to the Spirit shall of the Spirit reap life everlasting.—

then we see a rhetorical balance of similar syntactic arrangements which is plainly enough a rhythmic phenomenon. Such parallelisms appear both in phrases and in clauses—in Ben Jonson's "There was ever more in him to be praised than to be pardoned," and in Disraeli's "It is much easier to be critical than to be correct"; and, expanded, in Sir Thomas Browne's "Man is a noble animal, splendid in ashes and pompous in the grave," or Jeremy Taylor's "He that is choice of his time will also be choice of his company, and choice of his actions"; or simply, in Sidney's "There is no man suddenly either excellently good or extremely evil"; or more elaborately in Taylor's

For we must remember that we have a great work to do, many enemies to conquer, many evils to prevent, much danger to be run through, many difficulties to be mastered, many necessities to serve, and much good to do, many children to provide for, or many friends to support, or many poor to relieve, or many diseases to cure, besides the needs of nature and of relation, our private and our public cares, and duties of the world, which necessity and the providence of God hath adopted into the family of religion.

As with phrases, so with clauses, ranging from the simple "Youth is a blunder; manhood a struggle; old age a regret" (Disraeli) and "A witty woman is a treasure; a witty beauty is a power" (Meredith)—through the slightly different, though still simple "Kings will be tyrants from policy when subjects are rebels from principle" (Burke) and "The figure of a man may be a monster, but he is a solid monster. The figure of God may be a mistake, but it is an unmistakable mistake" (Chesterton) and "The Puritans hated bearbaiting, not because it gave pain to the bear, but because it gave pleasure to the spectators" (Macaulay)—to the longer and more complex:

The fact disclosed by a survey of the past that majorities have been wrong must not blind us to the complementary fact that majorities have usually not been entirely wrong.— Spencer.

Wherever literature consoles sorrow or assuages pain; wherever it brings gladness to eyes which fail with wakefulness and tears, and ache for the dark house and the long sleep,— there is exhibited in its noblest form the immortal influence of Athens.—Macaulay.

He often expressed his commiseration of Dryden's poverty, and his indignation at the age which suffered him to write for bread; he repeated with rapture the first lines of *All for Love*, but wondered at the corruption of taste which could bear anything so unnatural as rhyming tragedies.—Johnson.

In a favorite form of this parallelism the final member is expanded. This is, at its simplest, what Saintsbury (not too happily, but the name may stand in lieu of a better) called 'gradation'; as in "Where is the wise? where is the scribe? where is the disputer of this world?" (I Cor. 1: 20) or Landor's "Laodameia died; Helen died; Leda, the beloved of Jupiter, went before." The effect may be observed by comparing the illustrations; in the example from Disraeli there is something sharp and staccato, appropriate to the intention of the epigram, but not so pleasing to the ear as the protracted ending of the others, like the lengthened notes of a musical cadence. Or for a contrasting effect the third member may be shorter:

Softly beautiful are the tremulous shadows of leaves on the sunned sand; and the scent of flowers comes thinly sweet with every waft of tepid air; and there is a humming of bees.—Lafcadio Hearn.

Or there may be a cumulative series, in which the long last member is itself divided, as in Addison's essay on Westminster Abbey:

When I look upon the tombs of the great, every emotion of envy dies in me: when I read the epitaphs of the beautiful, every inordinate desire goes out: when I meet with the grief of parents upon a tombstone, my heart melts with compassion: when I see the tombs of the parents themselves, I consider the vanity of grieving for those whom we must quickly follow: when I see kings lying by those who deposed them, when I consider rival wits placed side by side, or the

holy men that divided the world with their contests and dis-
putes, I reflect with sorrow and astonishment on the little
competitions, factions, and debates of mankind.

These gradations show some other interesting varieties, in which the obvious rhythm is as it were veiled.[1]
These of Dryden's (on Chaucer) and Swift's (on Gar-
rick) are simple:

All his pilgrims are severally distinguished from each other;
and not only in their inclinations but in their very physiog-
nomies and persons.

His death eclipsed the gayety of nations, and impoverished
the public stock of harmless pleasure.

In this of Bishop South's both subject and object in the
last clause are expanded by a phrase, and in the second
clause the negative is put into a suffix:

Study was not then a duty, night-watchings were needless:
the light of reason wanted not the assistance of a candle.

This from William Lloyd Garrison (a common oratorical
form) expands the third member by a clause:

With reasonable men, I will reason; with humane men I will
plead; but to tyrants I will give no quarter, nor waste argu-
ments where they will certainly be lost.

In this from Burke the subject of the verb is graduated:
"The cheap defence of nations, the nurse of manly
sentiment and heroic enterprise, is gone." In this from
Carlyle it is the verb itself: "Every noble crown is, and
on earth will for ever be, a crown of thorns." In this
from Lytton Strachey there are three sections in each
member, with graduated variations:

The sisters were never separated for the whole of their long
lives. Agnes was cheerful, but of little value in the head;

she painted. Old Mr. Berry was cheerful, but quite incompetent; he did nothing at all. Mary was intelligent, with enough character for three at the very least; and she did everything that had to be done, with consummate ease.

Finally, in this from Ezekiel observe how curiously the four short clauses (the third itself graduated *up*, and the fourth *down* again) are balanced by the two short, or shorter, clauses, strengthened and lengthened with "behold" and "lo."

The hand of the Lord was upon me, and carried me out in the spirit of the Lord, and set me down in the midst of the valley which was full of bones, and caused me to pass by them round about, and behold, there were very many in the open valley, and lo, they were very dry.

All varieties of anaphora and similar figures, moreover, are sources of rhythmic effect, though not all in the same degree, for in some the repetition may be accompanied by such different matter that the feeling of the unit is lost.[2] Macaulay has an interesting variation:

The Life of Johnson is assuredly a great—a very great work. Homer is not more decidedly the first of heroic poets, Shakespeare is not more decidedly the first of dramatists, Demosthenes is not more decidedly the first of orators, than Boswell is the first of biographers. He has no second. He has distanced all his competitors so decidedly that it is not worth while to place them. Eclipse is first, and the rest nowhere.

To illustrate more fully—perhaps more fully than need be—the different kinds of balance and parallelism I submit the following specimens, with this observation (partly illustrative itself) from Ruskin:

In all perfectly beautiful objects there is found the opposition of one part to another and a reciprocal balance obtained. . . . Absolute equality is not required, still less absolute similarity. A mass of subdued colour may be balanced by a point of a powerful one, and a long and latent line overpowered by a short and conspicuous one.—*Modern Painters.*

This from Donne is tripartite, with gradation in the first member of each section, but the third member shortened by way of compensation:

One dieth at his full strength, being wholly at ease, and in quiet; and another dies in the bitterness of his soul and never eats with pleasure; but they all lie down alike in the dust and the worm covers them.

These two from Johnson need no comment, but the second is of interest as showing an appreciation of simplicity on the part of one who so often overplayed "the rhetorician's brass instrument":

All the other powers of literature are coy and haughty, they must long be courted, and at last are not always gained; but Criticism is a goddess easy of access, and forward of advance, who will meet the slow and encourage the timorous; the want of meaning she supplies with words, and the want of spirit she recompenses with malignity.—*Idler*, "Dick Minim the Critic."

Criticism, either didactic or defensive, occupies almost all his [Dryden's] prose, except those pages which he has devoted to his patrons; but none of his prefaces were ever thought tedious. They have not the formality of a settled style, in which the first half of the sentence betrays the other. The clauses are never balanced, nor the periods modelled: every word seems to drop by chance, though it falls into its proper place. Nothing is cold or languid; the whole is airy, animated, and vigorous; what is little is gay; what is great is splendid. He may be thought to mention himself too frequently; but while he forces himself upon our esteem, we cannot refuse him to stand high in his own. Everything is excused by the play of images and the spriteliness of expression. Though all is easy, nothing is feeble; though all seems careless, there is nothing harsh; and though since his earlier works more than a century has passed, they have nothing yet uncouth or obsolete.—"Life of Dryden."

The next illustration, from Landor's "Æsop and Rhodopé," is more subtly woven, the members are more varied; but the balance is carefully observed.[3]

Laodameia died; Helen died; Leda, the beloved of Jupiter, went before. It is better to repose in the earth betimes than to sit up late; better, than to cling pertinaciously to what we feel crumbling under us, and to protract an inevitable fall. We may enjoy the present, while we are insensible of infirmity and decay: but the present, like a note in music, is nothing but as it appertains to what is past and what is to come. There are no fields of amaranth on this side of the grave: there are no voices, O Rhodopé, that are not soon mute, however tuneful: there is no name, with whatever emphasis of passionate love repeated, of which the echo is not faint at last.

This opens with a simple gradation (already quoted). The next sentence turns on "better . . . than," the latter part of the comparison being protracted by additional modifiers. The third sentence has a simple balance ("enjoy the present . . . insensible of decay") varied by the extra phrase "of infirmity"; then "the present" is repeated, precisely "like a note in music." The final sentence comprises the threefold anaphora, with considerable expansion like the gradation of the first sentence. From such a sentence—and in order not to anticipate, the metrical adjuncts are passed over in silence—one can see what Landor meant when he wrote: "Good prose, to say nothing of the original thought it conveys, may be infinitely varied in modulation. It is only an extension of metres, and amplification of harmonies, of which even the best and most varied poetry admits but few."

Three further illustrations will more than suffice: a simple one (from Washington Irving), a more complex one, with inversions (from Vaughan), and a flamboyant one (from Macaulay)—

How many bright eyes grow dim—how many soft cheeks grow pale—how many lovely forms fade away into the tomb, and none can tell the cause of their blighted loveliness.

O pitiful and astonishing transformations. All is gone, all is dust, deformity and desolation. Their bones are scattered in the pit, and instead of well-set hair, there is baldness, and loathsomeness instead of beauty. This the state of their bodies, and (O blessed Jesus) who knows the state of their souls?

Death is there associated, not, as in Westminster Abbey and Saint Paul's, with genius and virtue, with public veneration and with imperishable renown; not, as in our humblest churches and churchyards, with everything that is most endearing in social and domestic charities; but with whatever is darkest in human nature and in human destiny, the savage triumph of implacable enemies, with the inconstancy, the ingratitude, the cowardice of friends, with all the miseries of fallen greatness and blighted fame.

It should be clear now that the repetition of syntactic parallelisms is a form of rhythm. However the parallel units may vary among themselves, however the content may differ provided the form is parallel, the repetition, so long as it is recognizable, is potential rhythm. Other rhythmic elements may complicate the picture—as will appear presently—but the sole point I wish to make here is that parallel construction, recognizably repeated, is the simple beginning of prose rhythm.[4]

The phrase, the clause, the sentence, the paragraph: in the first three it is not difficult to feel and follow what we are agreed in calling rhythm. How much farther will the ear, with the help perhaps of the eye, go in recognizing and responding to larger units? We shall probably do well not to press the question too hard, but we cannot evade it.

It has been said that Pater gave special attention to the rhythm of the paragraph; and Mr. Read goes so far as to say that the rhythm of sentences, which has been almost our sole interest hitherto, is nothing compared to that of paragraphs.[5] If this is true, we should now be at the summit of our study. Having tried as well as we could to understand the meaning and effect of sentence rhythm, we should now be prepared to take the next step, relate the minor rhythms of the successive sentences to one another and to the whole paragraph—and reach the peak. Yet this is not so easy to do. Small groups are readily felt and perhaps analyzed; it requires an attentive and a trained ear to follow the ebb and flow, the swell and subsidence, of sentence after sentence and perceive the unifying movement to which each part is duly subordinate; to catch the rhythmic impulse which begins with the first words of a paragraph and pursue its continuous course to the last words, where it arrives at its predetermined close. It not only requires an attentive and a trained ear, it implies that such a rhythm really exists, that all good writers construct their paragraphs with this ideal before them and succeed in attaining it. Or perhaps some do, and should be honored for it, while others do not and should be judged by the result.

Mr. Read exacts a high standard. "The sentences," he says,

must be dissolved in a wider movement and this wider movement is the rhythm of the paragraph—a rhythm that begins with the first syllable of the paragraph and is not complete without the last syllable. . . . It is born, not with the words, but with the thought, and with whatever confluence of instincts and emotions the thought is accompanied. As the thought takes shape in the mind, it takes a shape. . . . It exactly reproduces what we should call metaphorically the contour of our thought. The metaphor is for once exact: thought has a contour or shape. The paragraph is the perception of this contour or shape. (pp. 63, 65)

Mr. Read gives us several illustrations of this, but his comments are not altogether helpful. There is one paragraph from Emerson in which he says the sentences are rhythmic enough, while the paragraph leaves something to be desired, for the passage is a compilation from the *Journals*. There is another paragraph from Santayana, in which the separate sentences are well enough, but do not fuse into a paragraph; this often happens in the writing of foreigners. Or on the other side he instances a long passage from D. H. Lawrence's *Twilight in Italy*, in which "each paragraph is a complete action and reaction"; and from Milton's *Of Reformation in England* seven paragraphs, in which he finds "the mighty sweep of linked and modulated sounds" unbroken "from the first syllable to the last." The rhythm of Donne is "extremely elaborate, indeed intricate, full of returns and repetitions, of cadence and syllabic counterpoint." Traherne has "a sweetly modulated rhythm"; the "rhythmical structure" of Landor "is elaborate and even beautiful, but everything is sacrificed to this end." The gentle reader may respond eagerly to these observations, but the earnest analyst is hardly impressed. We are left with the feeling that paragraph rhythm is strictly speaking either a matter of metaphor or an illusion. The secret may still be, however, with Mr. Read. "In a sentence," he says, "the rhythm keeps close to the inner necessities of expression; it is determined in the act of creation. It is the natural modulation of the single cry." This is what he says of the paragraph also: "the contour of the thought." That is, for him all rhythm is "the natural modulation" of the substance of what is contained in the words: form and content fused—style. And on rhythm as style there will be something to say in a later chapter.

I cannot, however, leave Mr. Read and his mystical (I use the word cautiously, but in no pejorative sense) view of the matter without an effort to extract something helpful from what he offers—without submitting two of his illustrations to methodical analysis. Both of these he gives without particular comment, but as examples of the "wider movement" in which the rhythm "begins with the first syllable of the paragraph and is not complete without the last syllable." The first is the closing paragraph of Sir Thomas Browne's *Urn Burial*.

To subsist in lasting Monuments, to live in their productions, to exist in their names and predicament of chimeras, was large satisfaction unto old expectations, and made one part of their Elysiums. But all this is nothing in the Metaphysics of true belief. To live indeed is to be again ourselves, which being not only an hope but an evidence in noble believers, 'tis all one to lie in St. Innocent's churchyard, as in the sands or Aegypt; Ready to be anything, in the ecstasy of being ever, and as content with six foot as the Moles of Adrianus.

> tabesne cadavera solvat,
> An rogus, haud refert.—Lucan.

This is comparatively simple. The contour of the thought

is transparent: the pagan view (in three infinitive subject clauses with a compound predicate); the denial of it (in a simple sentence); the Christian view (in two short infinitive clauses, with a modifier in two parallel constructions); a restatement (also in parallel construction)—a rising curve, a peak, a slowly descending curve. The two curves are of approximately equal length, though their component groups are somewhat irregular; the second being prolonged by a coda, and finished off by a Latin flourish (not quoted by Mr. Read). The infinitives indicate the movement and continue it without offensive repetition; the coda completes them in a slightly varied form.

The second is from Mr. H. M. Tomlinson's *The Sea and the Jungle*. In this paragraph there is not, it seems to me, the same clearness of rhythm; the style is of course very different and so also is the contour of the thought; but do the curves flow harmoniously?

Full day came quickly to show me the reality of one of my early visions, and I suppose I may not expect many more such minutes as I spent when watching from the "Capella's" bridge the forest of the Amazon take shape. It was soon over. The morning light brimmed at the forest top, and spilled into the river. The channel filled with sunshine. There it was then. In the northern cliff I could see even the boughs and trunks; they were veins of silver in a mass of solid chrysolite. This forest had not the rounded and dull verdure of our own woods in midsummer, with deep bays of shadow. It was a sheer front, uniform, shadowless, and astonishingly vivid. I thought then the appearance of the forest was but a local feature, and so gazed at it for what it would show me next. It had nothing else to show me. Clumps of palms threw their fronds above the forest roof in some places, or a giant exogen raised a dome; but that was all. Those strong characters in the growth were seen only in passing. They did not change the outlook ahead

of converging lines of level green heights rising directly
from a brownish flood.[6]

The contour of the thought presents little difficulty:
an introductory statement (first sentence); the picture
revealed (four short sentences); the picture developed
(eight longer sentences, to the end)—to the north—contrast with English forest—description again—a personal
reflection—description again—summary. But admirable
and vivid as this is, one's first thought is that it is admirable and vivid because of its very informality. There is
an alternation of comment and description, but I discern
no movement initiated in the first syllables and progress-
ing to a predetermined conclusion. The first sentence belongs to a different world from the rest. There are none
of the syntactic repetitions which support the rhythmical
movement in the passage from Browne, nor any marked
arrangement of the sound groups.[7] On the other hand
there are many subtleties in the individual sentences which
exhibit lesser rhythms and contribute to the effect of flowing prose. There are numerous metrical runs, and such
combinations as "our own woods in midsummer, with
deep bays" and "Clumps of palms threw their fronds . . .
forest roof . . . raised a dome . . . that was all"; or the
longer "I thought then the ap- . . . and so gazed at it."
In the short sentences near the beginning there is a notable run of two- and three-stress groups which create a
larger rhythm. But all this is far from paragraph rhythm
in Mr. Read's sense.[8]

There is no injustice in taking only part of his example. In fact Mr. Read could have made out a better
case by taking three successive paragraphs: that which I
have quoted gives the 'still' picture; the next begins,

"Occasionally the river narrowed," and gives a near view; and the third, beginning "In some places the river widened into lagoons," completes it with a larger view. There is also a very cunning balance in the details at the end of the second and third paragraphs. Here they are without further comment:

Occasionally the river narrowed, or we passed close to one wall, and then we could see the texture of the forest surface, the microstructure of the cliff, though we could never look into it for more than a few yards, except where, in some places, habitations were thrust into the base of the woods, as in lower caverns. An exuberant wealth of forms built up that forest which was so featureless from a little distance. The numerous palms gave grace and life to the façade, for their plumes flung in noble arcs from tall and slender columns, or sprayed directly from the ground in emerald fountains. The rest was inextricable confusion. Vines looped across the front of green, binding the forest with cordage, and the roots of epiphytes dropped from upper boughs, like hanks of twine.

In some places the river widened into lagoons, and we seemed to be in a maze of islands. Canoes shot across the waterways, and river schooners, shaped very like junks, with high poops and blue and red sails, were diminished beneath the verdure, betraying the great height of the woods. Because of its longitudinal extension, fining down to a point in the distance, the elevation of the forest, when uncontrasted, looked much less than it really was. The scene was so luminous, still, and voiceless, it was so like a radiant mirage, or a vivid remembrance of an emotional dream got from books read and read again, that only the unquestionable verity of our iron steamer, present with her smoke and prosaic gear, convinced me that what was outside us was there. Across a hatch a large butterfly hovered and flickered like a flame. Dragon flies were suspended invisibly over our awning, jewels in shimmering enamels.

Inasmuch however as the question is one of some difficulty, and Mr. Read has a little disappointed us, we may well try a few more specimens. Take now the following paragraph of Macaulay's account of the siege of Londonderry.

May passed away: June arrived; and still Londonderry held out. There had been many sallies and skirmishes with various success: but, on the whole, the advantage had been with the garrison. Several officers of note had been carried prisoners into the city; and two French banners, torn after hard fighting from the besiegers, had been hung as trophies in the chancel of the Cathedral. It seemed that the siege must be turned into a blockade. But before the hope of reducing the town by main force was relinquished, it was determined to make a great effort. The point selected for assault was an outwork called Windmill Hill, which was not far from the southern gate. Religious stimulants were employed to animate the courage of the forlorn hope. Many volunteers bound themselves by oath to make their way into the works or to perish in the attempt. Captain Butler, son of the Lord Mountgarret, undertook to lead the sworn men to the attack. On the walls the colonists were drawn up in three ranks. The office of those who were behind was to load the muskets for those who were in front. The Irish came on boldly and with a fearful uproar, but after long and hard fighting were driven back. The women of Londonderry were seen amidst the thickest fire serving out water and ammunition to their husbands and brothers. In one place, where the wall was only seven feet high, Butler and some of his sworn men succeeded in reaching the top! but they were all killed or made prisoners. At length, after four hundred of the Irish had fallen, their chiefs ordered a retreat to be sounded.

The sentences, measured in words and in syllables, run thus:

WORDS:—10 (3 + 2 + 5)—21 (10 + 11)—33 (11 + 22)—11—21—19—12—19—16—11—18—19 (10 + 9)—20—31 (23 + 8)—18;

SYLLABLES:—15 (4 + 3 + 8)—31 (16 + 15)—51 (20 + 31)—13—29—25—21—26—22—13—21—26 (14 + 12)—33—39 (29 + 10)—25.

Neither of these forms of measurement is really adequate, and it would be a waste of ingenuity to force them to yield a series of definite proportions; yet the multiples of 10, or approximately 10, in the first series and the multiples of 5 in the second are noticeable; and the alternation of shorter and longer sentences in the middle of the paragraph is plain. On the whole the figures may be held to offer a fair index of what the ear 'feels,' namely, that there is an ordered flow of sounds not exactly measurable but rhythmically appreciable.

Here, next, are four consecutive paragraphs of almost equal length (69, 61, 59, 59 words each). Three of them consist of a short sentence followed by a longer one. And the "then" of the last paragraph helps to round out a continuous movement. Yet one hardly feels anything like paragraph-rhythm in the series. The eye recognizes them as four like-sized units on the page, but the ear does not receive or follow them as a succession of waves of sound, and this may be partly because each in itself is without a distinct flow of its own which can generate the sense of rhythm.

The initial obstacle to a sober-minded definition of Trollope's novels is that it provides a sensual rather than an intellectual experience. A smell, a pain or a sound is not more difficult to describe than the effect—at once soothing and exciting—produced on the reader's mind by the leisurely, nonchalant commentaries on English social life that carry his name on their title-pages.

The phenomenon is partly explicable by the fact that a Trollope novel is of the very essence of fiction. At its best it represents a distillation of that element in story-telling on which all other elements depend, without which no blend —however skilful—of fact, incident, idea and description can be recognized for fiction at all—the element of characterization.

There are novels more spiritual than his, more heroic and more beautiful; but there are none more faultless in this most delicate of all novel-writing problems. "Trollope" one critic has declared "is more than the painter or the sculptor of his people; he is the biographer of them all." That is high praise, but it is praise deserved.

Power of characterization, then, is the superlative quality of Trollope as a novelist. And as revealed by him, it is not a power of observation nor of imagination; not a power of knowledge nor of intuition; but a compound of all four, with a something added of the author's personality, giving to the whole a peculiar but elusive flavour.—Michael Sadleir, *Trollope; A Commentary*.

I am not sure that this next example exhibits what is properly called paragraph-rhythm. The movement is closely linked with the progression of ideas; and when I first read it I felt a rise and fall, a swing, a curve, which have at least a strong resemblance to rhythm. The author has been telling about *arroz a la Valenciana*, and says: "It takes a long time to make and is a great deal of trouble. But the best arroz I ever ate was at Tarragona." Then follows:

Tarragona has a cathedral that is grey and austere, very plain, with immense, severe pillars; it is like a fortress; a place of worship for headstrong, violent and cruel men. The night falls early within its walls and then the columns in the aisles seem to squat down on themselves and darkness shrouds the Gothic arches. It terrifies you. It is like a dungeon. I was there last on a Monday in Holy Week and from the pulpit a preacher was delivering a Lenten sermon. Two or three naked electric globes threw a cold light that cut the outline of the columns against the darkness as though with scissors. It only just fell upon the crowd, mostly women, who sat, between the chancel and the choir, huddled together as though they cowered in a fear of a foe that besieged the city. With violent gestures, in a loud, scolding voice, the preacher poured forth with extreme rapidity a torrent of denunciation. Each angry, florid phrase was like a blow and one blow followed another with vicious insistence. From the farthest end of the majestic church, winding about the columns and curling round the groining of the arches, down the great austere nave and along the dungeon-like aisles, that rasping, shrewish voice pursued you.

But a devout admirer had entertained the preacher at luncheon that day in the hotel in which I was staying. It was quite a party. There were the host's grey-haired and corpulent wife, his two sons with their wives, or his two daughters with their husbands (I could only guess), and eight or nine children of various ages, whom I tried to sort out. The preacher tucked in to the arroz like one o'clock. It comforted me at that moment to remember this. It was a bad, bad world, but a merciful providence had allowed occasional alleviations to the miserable lot of man, and among these must undoubtedly be placed arroz a la Valenciana as we had both eaten it that noon at Tarragona.—W. Somerset Maugham, *Don Fernando*.

The tune is called before the piece begins. Then we swing away on the grim picture of the cathedral; a new wave starts with "I was there last"—the harsh interior, the cowering crowd, the violent preacher; and a finale in which the torrential denunciations interweave themselves among the aisles and arches. But we know there is more to come, for we have not reached the *arroz*. The new paragraph opens accordingly with the conjunction; another, contrasting picture is presented, with its clustering details; the first and second vignettes are brought together; and the grand finale brings full satisfaction, with subdominant and dominant—"arroz" and "Tarragona." A little feeling of contrivance there may be, but the whole is so gracefully contrived and so delicately spiced that we condone the artifice.

In the first two editions of Volume I of *Modern Painters* there was a very long paragraph[9] with a kind of inner rhythm based on a succession of names: Claude, Salvator, Poussin, David Cox, Copley Fielding, J. D. Harding, Clarkson Stanfield, culminating with "And Turner." This was followed, after a transition on Canaletto, by a series of paragraphs beginning "Let us pass to Prout"—"Let us take Stanfield then"—"But let us take Turner"—ending with "Yes, Mr. Turner, we are in Venice now," which is a paragraph by itself. The proper names within the first long paragraph are nearly equally spaced; they catch the eye as one reads and prepare the attention for the series which follows with its "let us" refrain. The method may be obvious, but without pointers the effect might have been missed.

A still more striking use of the same technique, but with the refrain at the end, is to be found in Part II, section 3, chapter iv, of the same volume. It is also a long paragraph, but worth quoting not only as an illustration of the sustained long-unit rhythm, but as a specimen, full of its own various and lesser rhythms, of the Ruskinian purple, which he himself regarded as "perhaps the best and truest piece of work" in the volume. I omit the first dozen lines and take the liberty of italicizing the refrain.

Stand upon the peak of some isolated mountain at daybreak, when the night mists first rise from off the plains, and watch their white and lake-like fields, as they float in level bays and winding gulfs about the islanded summits of the lower hills, untouched yet by more than dawn, colder and more quiet than a windless sea under the moon of midnight; watch when the first sunbeam is sent upon the silver channels, how the foam of their undulating surface parts and passes away, and down under their depths the glittering city and green pasture lie like Atlantis, between the white paths of winding rivers; the flakes of light falling every moment faster and broader among the starry spires, as the wreathed surges break and vanish above them, and the confused crests and ridges of the dark hills shorten their grey shadows upon the plain. *Has Claude given this?* Wait a little longer, and you shall see those scattered mists rallying in the ravines, and floating up towards you, along the winding valleys, till they crouch in quiet masses, iridescent with the morning light, upon the broad breasts of the higher hills, whose leagues of massy undulation will melt back and back into that robe of material light, until they fade away, lost in its lustre, to appear again above, in the serene heaven, like a wild, bright, impossible dream, foundationless and inaccessible, their very bases vanishing in the unsubstantial and mocking blue of the deep lake below. *Has Claude given this?* Wait yet a little longer, and you shall see those mists gather themselves into white towers, and stand like fortresses among the promontories, massy and motionless, only piled with every instant higher and higher into the sky, and casting longer shadows athwart the rocks; and out of the pale blue of the horizon you will see forming and advancing a troop of narrow, dark, pointed vapours, which will cover the sky, inch by inch, with their grey network, and take the light off the landscape with an eclipse which will stop the singing of the birds and the motion of the leaves, together; and then you will see horizontal bars of black shadow forming under them, you know not how, along the shoulders of the hills; you never see them form, but when you look back to a place which was clear an instant ago, there is a cloud on it, hanging by the precipices, as a hawk pauses over his prey. *Has Claude given this?* And then you will hear the sudden rush of the awakened wind, and you will see those watch-towers of vapour swept away from their foundations, and waving curtains of opaque rain let down to the valleys, swinging from the burdened clouds in black bending fringes, or pacing in pale columns along the lake level, grazing its surface into foam as they go. And then, as the sun sinks, you shall see the storm drift for an instant from off the hills, leaving their broad sides smoking, and loaded yet with snow-white, torn, steam-like rags of capricious vapour, now gone, now gathered again; while the smouldering sun, seeming not far away, but burning like a red-hot ball beside you, and as if you could reach it, plunges through the rushing wind and rolling cloud with headlong fall, as if it meant to rise no more, dyeing all the air about it with blood. *Has Claude given this?* And then you shall hear the fainting tempest die in the hollow of the night, and you shall see a green halo kindling on the summit of the eastern hills, brighter—brighter yet, till the large white circle of the slow moon is lifted up among the barred clouds, step by step, line by line; star after star she quenches with her kindling light, setting in their stead an army of pale, penetrable, fleecy wreaths in the heaven, to give light upon the earth, which move together, hand in hand, company by company, troop by troop, so measured in their unity of motion, that the whole heaven seems to roll with them, and the earth to reel under them. *Ask Claude, or his brethren, for that.* And then wait yet for one hour, until the east again becomes purple, and the heaving mountains, rolling against it in darkness, like waves of a wild sea, are drowned one by one in the glory of its burning: watch the white glaciers blaze in their winding paths about the mountains, like mighty serpents with scales of fire: watch the columnar peaks of solitary snow, kindling downwards, chasm by chasm, each in itself a new morning; their long avalanches cast down in keen streams brighter than the lightning, sending each his tribute of driven snow, like altarsmoke, up to the heaven; the rose-light of their silent domes flushing that heaven about them and above them, piercing with purer light through its purple lines of lifted cloud, casting a new glory on every wreath as it passes by, until the whole heaven, one scarlet canopy, is interwoven with a roof of waving flame, and tossing, vault beyond vault, as with the drifted wings of many companies of angels: and then, when you can look no more for gladness, and when you are bowed down with fear and love of the Maker and Doer of this, tell me who has best delivered this His message unto men!

IV

Rhythm and Meter

i

IT GOES WITHOUT SAYING that the words of our English language fall easily into metrical patterns, else it would go hard with the poets when they undertake to write in verse. Whether this tendency to a regularity which approaches the regularity of verse is inherent in the language, or is accidental, or is a development, an adjustment gradually worked out to comfort the ear, or is even due in some part to the reverse influence of verse itself: these are debatable points. But it surprises no one to observe frequently in English prose a series of metrical feet which amounts to a verse movement. This latent meter sometimes exists without being recognized either by the writer or by the reader, and sometimes on the other hand becomes so prominent as to be a distraction. It is sometimes unintentional and sometimes deliberate. As most critics admit, metrical passages are not in themselves a sin against prose; for in fact they are nearly unavoidable. The offense comes when the meter obtrudes itself on the attention as a meretricious ornament or when the regularity is so strong as to disturb the feeling of prose and substitute the feeling of verse. So long as the prose rhythm remains intact, undisplaced by the verse, or displaced only for a moment, there is no harm. Aristotle made this observation; it has been repeated many times, for example: "Both movements are there, and we hear verse through the prose just as we hear prose through Shakespeare's verse. Two distinct pleasures are interwoven but not confounded."[1]

What Saintsbury calls "the beautiful bane of blank verse"—the phrase is not without its own little tune—has been found repeatedly in all the writers of formal prose from Chaucer's "Melibeus" down to the present. Even a learned lecturer like Professor Kittredge, reaching a high point in his exposition of the Pardoner's character, drops into poetry, no doubt unawares;[2] Burke, Dr. Brown (in *Rab and His Friends*), Dickens in his pathetic passages, Blackmore, Swinburne, and Ruskin are notable purveyors of this contraband. The experiments at the close of Kingsley's *Hypatia* and Charlotte Brontë's *Vilette* are well known. Two specimens of the worser sort will do here:

Life is a narrow vale between the cold and barren peaks of two verities. We strive in vain to look beyond the heights. We cry aloud—and the only answer is the echo of our wailing cry. From the voiceless lips of the unreplying dead there comes no word. But in the night of Death Hope sees a star and listening Love can hear the rustling of a wing.

So in this land of long, long winter night, where nature stints her joys for six hard months, then owns her debt and pays it all at once, the spring is glorious compensation for the past, six months' arrears of joy are paid in one vast lavish outpour.[3]

Even stanzas may be found. The prime exhibit in this kind is the often quoted

> And so no force, however great,
> 　can strain a cord, however fine,
> 　into a horizontal line
> that shall be absolutely straight.[4]

Ruskin in his description of Rouen has:

> And the city lay
>   under its guarding hills
>   one labyrinth of delight,
>   its grey and fretted towers
>   misty in their magnificence of height;

where the omission of "magnificence of" makes the stanza recognizable. And close thereafter:

> And the (far-reaching) ridges of pastoral mountain
>   (succeed each other)
>   like the long and sighing swell
>   which moves over quiet waters,
>   from some far-off stormy sea.

where the omission of the parenthesized words gives us a tolerable quatrain, without rime but with alternating feminine and masculine endings—to say nothing of the lilt of "the far-reaching ridges of pastoral mountain." Macaulay has a rough ballad stanza, unrimed, in chapter ii of his *History:*

> There were gentlemen and there were seamen
>   in the navy of Charles II.
> But the seamen were not gentlemen,
>   and the gentlemen were not seamen;

and part of one lurks in

> Vice itself lost half its evil,
>   by losing all its grossness.
>   —Burke

There is a little rimed stanza in Lincoln's Second Inaugural:

> Fondly do we hope,
>   fervently do we pray,

that this mighty scourge of war
   may speedily pass away.

The opening of the Lord's Prayer is in the form of an unrimed limerick:

Our father which art in heaven
Hallowed be thy name
   thy kingdom come
   thy will be done
on earth as it is in heaven.

Dr. MacColl drew attention to the stanza movement at the beginning of Bacon's essay "Of Parents and Children":

The joys of parents are secret
   and so are their griefs and fears:
they cannot utter the one,
   nor they will not utter the other.

Children sweeten labours,
   but they make misfortune more bitter;
they increase the cares of life,
   but they mitigate the remembrance of death.

There may be a slight falling off in the second stanza; but not everyone thinks of the Lord Chancellor as a poet.

Rime may be accidental in prose or deliberate, and between the two extremes lie, as usual, various gradations. Examples are everywhere. For the purely accidental take Newman's (from the *Apologia*): "As to Dr. Whately, his mind was too different from mine for us to remain long on one line." In Hardy's (from *Two on a Tower*) "The masses of hair that were once darkness visible had become touched here and there by a faint grey haze like the Via Lactea in a midnight sky," the rimes of "hair" and "there" (and perhaps "were") are apparently unintentional, but the molossus, "faint grey haze," has a conscious air and the long *i*'s at the end are suggestive of deliberate artistry. In Trollope's (from the *Auto-biography*)

If I could do this, then I thought I might succeed in impregnating the mind of the novel-reader with a feeling that honesty is the best policy; that truth prevails while falsehood fails; that a girl will be loved. . .

the jingle is probably a tag. But the intention is overt, and even notified to the reader, in Meredith's (from *Vittoria*)

"Right, my dear Ugo," said Agostino, turning round to him; "and I will then compose his hymn of praise. He has swallowed enough of Austrian bread. He took an Austrian wife to his bed. Who knows? he may some day declare a preference for Austrian lead. But we shall have to follow him, or stay at home drivelling."

And the satiric criticism is maliciously obvious in Maginn's parody of Disraeli:

O reader dear! do pray look here, and you will spy the curly hair, and forehead fair, and nose so high, and gleaming eye, of Benjamin Disraeli, the wondrous boy who wrote *Alroy* in rhyme and prose, only to show how long ago victorious Judah's lion-banner rose.[5]

Finally, one turns to Swinburne for a bravura illustration. In his review article on Locker Lampson's *Lyra Elegantiarum* (the *Forum* for October 1891) Swinburne ends a page-long, apparently serious paragraph with:

Literary history will hardly care to remember or to register the fact that there was a bad poet named Clough, whom his friends found it useless to puff; for the public, if dull, has not quite such a skull as belongs to believers in Clough.

It would be easy to draw up a graduated scale with verse at one end and prose at the other, between which will lie various hybrid forms containing to a greater or less degree the marks of either pure form. Terms have been suggested for certain rough divisions: (1) *characteristic verse,* in which the metrical pattern is plain and is followed with noticeable closeness; (2) *verse invaded by prose emphasis* (which might be called free verse if the phrase had not already been applied to a special historical phenomenon) in which the metrical pattern is still predominant, but is less insisted upon; (3) *numerous prose* (polyphonic is a more recent and more poetic denomination), in which the prose has been invaded by metrical patterns, distinctly noticeable and fairly consistent, but not offensive to the ear; and (4) *characteristic prose,* with no overt suggestions of meter—beyond of course what is inherent in our language.[6] The first two are not our present concern: there are difficulties enough in the others.

Such a classification implies no fundamental distinction between the rhythm of verse and that of prose: the difference is only in degree of regularity. Perfect regularity is found only in the abstract metrical pattern, and by the nature of speech sounds it is extremely rare if not actually impossible in language. But in verse the regularity is of such a high degree as to be always expected and nearly always recognized, though the poet carefully avoids an excess of this virtue and by variation enhances the value of what he seems to eschew. Then from the systematic regularity of verse there proceed in a descending scale continual degrees of more and more striking variation, till a point is reached where practically no regularity at all is recognizable. This other extreme, however, is as nearly impossible in language as the first, since there probably exists no sentence of any length, no logical arrangement of words, which is completely a-rhythmic and which does not contain some recognizable pattern at least latent. *See the cat* and *The boy has a drum* not only are scannable and can be fitted into verse, but their rhythmic potentiality is of the same stuff whether they are found in prose or in verse. There is, to be sure, one rhythm of verse and another of prose, but they have the same parentage, and they differ only in the fact that the one is highly organized to a predetermined pattern, while the other is not. In one sense, prose is ever *becoming* verse, but unintentionally, unwillingly; while verse is ever *becoming* prose, but purposely and purposefully. In another sense, prose can never *be* verse unless it is deliberately set to meter, and verse can never *be* prose unless it consciously abandons its plan of being metrical—that is, unless they both belie their own character. But there could not be this mutual attraction of one to the other if they were not both made of the same material.

It has seemed necessary to insist on this point, for it enables us to say clearly that when we find and point out metrical or quasi-metrical passages in ordinary prose, their metrical character may be of the nature of an 'accident,' an accident resulting from the way in which our words and phrases fall of themselves into regular patterns, and from an inherent desire of all users of English which is not satisfied without rhythmical patterns and to some degree has actually forced our words and phrases into these very patterns.[7]

To turn now from the theoretical to the practical, and try to find a way of profitably analyzing these metrical fragments or sequences of feet in their relation to the rhythm of a sentence. There are two dangers. One is that because we are looking for meter we may easily force the evidence and find it where it hardly exists. This is partly a matter of individual judgment. Swinburne's

> From her stainless and Olympian summit
> Of divine and indifferent light

seems to Professor Saintsbury an example of "pure prose rhythm"; only when the "and's" are removed does he feel the verse movement.[8] But to my ear the metrical regularity is at once obvious: two anapestic verses of three beats each, quite as regular as

> I have passed from the outermost portal
> To the shrine where a sin is a prayer;

and more regular than many other lines of *Dolores*. The extra syllable in the second anapest may be paralleled in

> Though the fol*iage be sod*den with tears.

Many a line of blank verse, taken by itself, would read more like prose than like verse—

> See where Christ's blood streams in the firmament. . .
> Of man's first disobedience, and the fruit. . .

Shall we say that these are not metrical? If not, to what limits can we safely go in finding blank verse lines in prose? Pope's

> Most women have no character at all

is as natural a prose sentence as could be; yet it is also a five-beat iambic line. Carlyle's famous dictum that "History is the essence of innumerable biographies" is above suspicion as plain prose, yet with no more synizesis than is common in ordinary speech and in verse also *(hist'ry,*

innum'rable) it is a sequence of four regular feet—to give
them classical names, three first pæons and a dactyl. Shall
we call Pope's sentence metrical and Carlyle's not, merely
because one appears in a verse context and the other in
prose?

The second danger is to assume that where we discover metrical inlays they are consciously contrived by the
writer as adornments of his style, whereas the fact may be
quite to the contrary. It is often easier to write scraps of
verse, with alliterative jingles and even rime, than to
write proper, well-sounding prose. Every careful writer is
aware of the necessity of casting out these too-facile 'beauties' by diligent revision. The wonder is not that so-and-
so writes 'rhythmical prose,' but rather that he avoids
a too obvious regularity, a monotonous jog trot, with
metrical flourishes which are unsuitable and offensive.
Some of the passages quoted earlier in this chapter will
serve as examples.

These dangers are perhaps not serious, but they need
to be recognized, and they may properly be borne in
mind in the course of the following analyses.

To the seventeenth-century writers of numerous prose
we turn most naturally for examples. Take first the famous finale of Raleigh's *History of the World*.

O eloquent, just, and mighty Death: whom none could
advise, thou hast persuaded; what none hath dared thou
hast done; and whom all the world hath flattered, thou
only hast cast out of the world and despised. Thou hast
drawn together all the far-stretched greatness, all the pride,
cruelty, and ambition of man, and covered it all over with
these two narrow words, *Hic jacet*.

Surely there is no prominence of meter in this; Saintsbury says expressly that it "never trenches upon verse";

and I should be the first to admit that its rhythmic secrets
are not wholly revealed by scansion. But let us see. It
begins with four four-beat lines, the second of which has
a so-called inversion at the medial pause and a feminine
ending, and the third a missing light syllable at the pause:

O eloquent, just, and mighty Death!

whom none could advise, thou hast persuaded;

what none hath dared, thou has done;

and whom all the world has flattered, thou. . .

The sentence ends with two anapests, "of the world and
despised" (which are repeated in the next sentence by
"and ambition of man"). Then follows a blank verse
with feminine ending:

Thou has drawn together all the far-stretched greatness;

and after a little the four-beat line:

and covered it all over with these

like the third line. The meter is certainly subdued, but
it is there, carrying throughout a secondary movement
beneath the balance of clauses which constitutes the primary rhythm.

Take the equally fine passage from Donne, which I
shall try later to analyze by another method:

If some kíng of the éarth have so lárge an extént
of domínion in nórth and sóuth
às that he háth wínter and súmmer
togéther in hìs domínions;
so lárge an extént éast and wést
às that he háth dáy and níght
togéther in hìs domínions,

> much móre hath Gód mércy and jústice
> togéther. He broúght líght out of dárkness,
>   nót out of a lésser líght;
> He can bríng thy súmmer oút of wínter . . .

a fairly regular series of three- and four-beat lines, with
the same kind of inversion or clash of accent as in the
passage from Raleigh.

Consider another famous set piece, that at the close
of Sir Thomas Browne's *Urn Burial*, where the series is
one of three- and two-beat lines:

> What sóng the Sýrens sáng,
> or what náme Achílles assúmed
> when he híd himsélf among wómen,
>   though púzzling quéstions,
> are nót beyond áll conjécture.
> What tíme the pérsons of thòse
> óssuaries éntered the fámous
>   nátions of the déad,
> and slépt with prínces and cóunsellors,
> might admít a wíde solútion. . . .

And note also the blank verse: "entered the famous nations of the dead."

After these illustrations, in which the numerous quality, though not precisely the metrical, is conscious and to
some degree deliberate, turn to the more difficult ones
where the metrical runs are less continuous and the movement less expected. "With a higher moral nature," says
Spencer in his *First Principles*, "will come a restriction on
the multiplication of the inferior." This begins with a
four-beat trochaic line:

> Wíth a hígher móral náture,

after which follows an iambic-dactylic sequence, "wĭll

´　˘　˘　´　　　　　　　　　　　　　　˘
come a restrict-," which is at once duplicated with "the

`　˘　˘　´
multiplica-"; the rest is prose. "Evil," says the same author, "perpetually tends to disappear": two dactyls and three iambs. "A woman with fair opportunities and without a positive hump," says Thackeray, "may marry whom she likes": three dactyls—anapest, iamb, anapest—three iambs. "Perfect simplicity is unconsciously audacious" (Meredith): two dactyls and the falling rhythm continued with long dactyls and a trochee. "His conversation does not show the minute-hand, but he strikes the hour very correctly" (Dr. Johnson): the first clause is a tolerable alexandrine, as good as, or even smoother than, Shelley's

> As from thy presence showers a rain of melody . . .
> The silence of that heart's accepted sacrifice . . .
> Consuming the last clouds of cold mortality . . .
> Beacons from the abode where the Eternal are.

"He strikes the hour" is two iambs; the last is a *cursus planus*.[9]

Saintsbury (p. 231) quotes as an example of conversational tone, in which meaning is the governing principle of the rhythm—by which I understand that *sound* is *not* the governing principle—this sentence of Cowley's:

There is no saying shocks me so much as that which I hear very often: that a man does not know how to pass his time.

Perhaps the meter is not very obvious at first; but note the trochees in "saying shocks me" and "very often," the iambs in "so much as that" and "to pass his time," and the anapests in "which I hear very oft-." Observe further that in rapid reading the strong emphasis on "no" tends to lessen the stress on "saying" and the movement becomes anapestic: "There is no saying shocks me so much. . ." Observe the same phenomenon in "hear" and "very." Now omit the two introductory syllables, and you have a passable dactylic hexameter—

> No saying shocks me so much as that which I
> hear very often.

Finally, read the whole sentence with these notations in mind, and it all becomes clearly rhythmic; in fact, one should say, the metrical base becomes clear. This process may seem at first like reading a foreign tune into the sentence, or forcing one upon the sentence. But it is not so. The meter is there. The sentence is of course not altogether metrical, for Cowley was writing prose, not verse. Yet it would be wrong to deny the latent meter just because the pattern was not obvious at first. For if one is unwilling to recognize this principle of the rhythmic undertone, if one is unwilling to hear and feel this organization of sounds, this rise and fall of accents, this undulation, beneath the surface, one must be ready to repudiate an important aspect of prose rhythm.

Another example from Professor Saintsbury. "What possible harmony or rhythmical effect," he asks (p. 240), "can you get out of the jerky vulgarity of Rymer's 'Fancy leaps and frisks, and away she's gone'?" Well, one may ask in turn: is it not almost too metrical? Try it as a five-beat trochaic line catalectic (to speak pedantically), not too smooth perhaps, but with a trisyllabic fourth foot for speed. Or try it to a different tune, like "Seasons come and go, and the summer's past" or "Flowers bloom and fade, and the year speeds on"; and you have a form of dipodic verse like Meredith's

> Wavy in the dusk lit by one large star . . .
> Jasmine winds the porch with stars two and three.

Or take the splendid sentence of Glanvill's: "Man does not yield himself to the angels, nor unto death utterly, save only through the weakness of his feeble will." The latter half is, says Saintsbury (p. 202, n. 1), "by itself almost insolently metrical." (It suggests dipodic verse, again.) The tautological "feeble," which he noted also, obviates a blank verse which would be inharmonious with the movement of the whole, though it leaves an alexandrine. But "the entirely different opening . . . reclaims and redeems it for prose." This is true, yet behind the prose is something almost metrical:

> Man doth not yield himself
> to the angels, nor unto death
> utterly, save only . . .

More examples of this sort could easily be given. I shall be satisfied, however, if I have shown that metrical sequences are to be found—not everywhere, but in unexpected places. I must continue nevertheless with a few instances of a somewhat different type. One does not need to scan in order to find the meter in this sentence from Henry Kingsley's *Ravenshoe:*

Up in his room he could hear that the wind was worse than ever, not rushing up in great gusts and sinking again, as in ordinary gales, but keeping up one continued unvarying scream against the house, which was terrible to hear.

And the same is true of this, from Blackmore's *Cristowell:*

But the play of lighter colours also, and the glimpse of silver stems, arise around the craggy openings, and birth of some fern-cradled rill. Far in the depth, short loops of water flash, like a clue to the labyrinth.

Yet Blackmore was not content with this flow of sweet sound. For three years later (1885) he revised the passage, elaborating the distinctly metrical effects, no doubt because they pleased him or because he thought they would please others:

But the play of lighter colours and the glimpse of silver stems enliven the verge of a shingled clearing, or birth of some fern-cradled rill. Deep in the wooded bottom quiver, like a clue of gossamer, sunny threads of twisted river, wafted through the lifts of gloom.[10]

Here, on the other hand, is a bit of Thackeray (the *Roundabout Papers,* "On a Lazy Idle Boy"), one amorphous sentence as wandering as the thing it describes, filled with varied sequences meant perhaps to underline the "sweet pretty" picture, and even adorned (if the word is not too sarcastic) with a rimed couplet. I will not go through it with analytical pointer, but merely suggest that it be read first lightly, then slowly with full attention to all the metrical potentialities, and finally lightly again, but with a memory of the undersound of all the little tunes. How much of this is mere playfulness and how much Thackeray expected us to take seriously it would be rash to inquire.

There was a sweet pretty river walk we used to take in the evening and mark the mountains round gloaming with a deeper purple; the shades creeping up the golden walls; the river brawling, the cattle calling, the maids round the fountains babbling and bawling; and several times in the course of our sober walks, we overtook a lazy slouching boy, a hobbledehoy, with a rusty coat, trousers not too long, and big feet trailing lazily one after the other, and large lazy hands dawdling from out the tight sleeves, and in the lazy hands a little book, which my lad held up to his face, and which I daresay so charmed and ravished him, that he was blind to the beautiful sights around him; unmindful I would venture to lay any wager, of the lessons he had to learn to-morrow; forgetful of mother waiting supper, and father preparing a scolding;—absorbed utterly and entirely in his book.

My next sample, perhaps unexpectedly, is a para-graph from *Romola:*

About the time when the two Campagnacci went on their errand, there was another man who, on the opposite side of the Arno, was also going out into the chill grey twilight. His errand, apparently, could have no relation to theirs; he was making his way to the brink of the river at a spot which, though within the city walls, was overlooked by no dwell-ings, and which only seemed the more shrouded and lonely for the warehouses and granaries which at some little dis-tance backward turned their shoulders to the river. There was a sloping width of long grass and rushes made all the more dank by broad gutters which here and there emptied themselves into the Arno.

The first three words make two iambs, the words coin-ciding with the feet. More noticeable are the dactyls (with two trochees): "time when the two Campagnacci went on their errand"; and this dactylic movement is car-ried further by "opposite side of the Arno, was . . . into the grey chill twilight. His . . . errand apparently . . . -lation to . . . making his way to the brink of the river at . . . shrouded and lonely for . . . -houses and granaries . . . some little . . . shoulders to." And with this dactylic movement there is a long iambic sequence: "which, though within the city walls was overlooked by no . . . which only seemed the more"; and a little later a trochaic sequence, "distance backward turned their shoulders . . . river." The third sentence is only a little less metrical; but I for-bear the analysis. Surely George Eliot will not be ac-

cused of being one of those stylists who consciously debase
their prose with meretricious metrical adornment; or, on
the other hand, one who cultivated numerous prose; but
rather one who permitted the metrical nature of the language to betray her sometimes into a kind of singsong.

The foregoing analyses are presented with a certain
hesitation. They will not commend themselves to all
readers. Nor will all of them, certainly, be equally clear
or persuasive; for, as I have said, each of us reads with
different emphases, and it is one of the characteristics of
a sequence that it makes use, as all verse does, of secondary stresses which one reader will take with more and
another with less attention. Yet they may have some
value in an effort to understand what there is which gives
us the impression of rhythm in sentences where the key
is not obvious. They should not be taken too literally:
no one, I trust, would pronounce some of the sentences
as I have 'scanned' them, for the scansion is only a basis
of rhythm, not the rhythm itself. Just as the metrical
pattern of verse does not represent the actual reading,
but the theoretic norm to which the language of verse is
adjusted, so these submetrical patterns of prose rhythm
represent—only at what one might call two removes—an
underlying scheme, usually unconscious on the part of
the writer in the sense that they were not aimed at, yet
existent in the sense that they reveal themselves to the
attentive ear.

ii

One of the great differences between prose and verse
is the greater speed, or apparent speed, of the former and
its greater variability of tempo. In verse underneath all
the changes of time and stress determined by the meaning

and the emotion there is the quiet tempering beat of the metronome, which like the governor of a machine steadies the movement. Not exactly, of course, but in a way not known to prose. These changes of tempo are in part due to the different purposes and functions of prose and in part also to its greater flexibility.

An important aspect of this difference has frequently been noticed by the prosodists. A verse of five metrical beats may have less than five prose or rhetorical emphases. For example there are five in

> The curfew tolls the knell of parting day;

there are four in

> Much have I travelled in the realms of gold.
>
> Of man's first disobedience and the fruit;

there are three in

> Silent, upon a peak in Darien.
>
> The weariness, the fever, and the fret;

there are two in

> In which the burden of the mystery.
>
> Than that you should remember, and be sad.
>
> As if predestination over-ruled;

and (to make all neat) here is a tolerable verse, invented for the nonce, with one—

> Or of the imperceptibility.

It is characteristic of prose to take the unemphatic syllables lightly, passing over the secondary accents of long words and the lesser rhetorical stresses with hardly more attention than it gives to the wholly unstressed, just as it is a characteristic of verse to emphasize them as a source of variation from the metronomic regularity. This makes for a kind of swiftness in prose which is almost beyond the range of verse.[11] But there is a corollary which says that in verse trisyllabic feet make for greater speed than disyllabic feet, that anapests and dactyls go faster than iambs and trochees; and however this may be by mechanical measurement it certainly is true as a matter of impression. Trisyllabic feet *seem* ordinarily to go faster. Now the absolute proportion of multisyllabic 'feet' in prose has been established by count and has been made a real criterion of prose rhythm by one school of research. The details may be relegated to a footnote.[12] A single short example will tell the whole story: the brisk opening sentence from one of Mr. J. B. Priestley's tales:

"And thank *you*," said the landlady, with the mechanical cheerfulness of her kind.

It has six stressed syllables to fourteen unstressed, or a ratio of 70 per cent unstressed.

But it must be insisted that even when such statistics (as in note twelve) are gathered on a large scale, they can afford only one index of prose rhythm, its rapidity, or rather tempo. The comparison with verse is a secondary matter. The greater the proportion of light syllables the faster the sentences seem to go; and conversely, since attention is an important factor in the perception of rhythm, the more slowly a sentence seems to *want* to go, that is, when the meaning or the feeling retards the reading, the more prominent will the latent metrical rhythm become, and concomitantly the more marked will the secondary or potential stresses tend to become. But that this *is* one index of rhythm will hardly be disputed.

Here are, for a conclusion, two examples of conversational prose.

The truth of it is, that a man in much business must either make himself a knave, or else the world will make him a fool: and, if the injury went no farther than the being laughed at, a wise man would content himself with the revenge of the retaliation; but the case is much worse, for these civil cannibals too, as well as the wild ones, not only dance about such a taken stranger, but at last devour him. A sober man cannot get too soon out of drunken company, though they be never so kind and merry among themselves; 'tis not unpleasant only, but dangerous to him. (Cowley)

This certainly goes at a quick tempo. For example, in the iambic sequence "must either make himself a knave" and the corresponding "or else the world will make him a fool" one brings out the contrast by special emphasis on "knave," "world," "fool," and thereby so reduces the metrically potential stresses that the latent meter is barely heard; and in the next clause one stresses "in-" and "wise," subordinating the trochaic sequence "farther than the being laughed at"; and similarly, again, with the dactylic sequence "though they be never so kind and merry among themselves." Thus is created a sort of counterpoint of two rhythms which are the result of two tempos: either can be brought out at will, but the sense and tone of the passage determines the quicker movement.

The other example is from Dryden's Preface to the *Fables*.

What júdgment I hád, incréases rather than dimínishes; and thóughts, such as they áre, come crówding ín so fást upon me, that my ónly dífficulty is to chóose or to rejéct, to rún them into vérse, or to gìve them the óther hármony of próse: I have so lóng stúdied and práctised bóth, that they are grówn in to a hábit, and become famíliar to me. In shórt, though I may láwfully pléad sóme pàrt of the òld géntleman's excúse, yet I will resérve it till I think I have gréater néed, and ásk nó graíns of allówance for the faúlts of thís my présent wórk, but thóse which are gìven of cóurse to húman fraílty.

Here you would say is a man *talking*. But though the passage reads and sounds like skilful improvising, it comes from one who says he has studied and practiced the writing of prose for a long time, and from one whose prose is in its kind still unsurpassed. You would not mark it, reading it with attention to what it says, as conspicuous for rhythm, yet there are some interesting curiosities in it. I have scanned it several times, with the result that it seems to contain between 66 per cent and 70 per cent of unstressed syllables (the latter figure as I have accented it above)—the variation coming from the speed with which it is read and the attention given to subordinate stresses.

NOTE ON CADENCE AND THE CURSUS

The *cursus* is an historical phenomenon starting with the Greek orators, adopted by Cicero, and spreading into medieval Latin under Ciceronian influence. It meant the use of certain quantitative feet (in medieval Latin, their accentual equivalents) at the ends of clauses and sentences. 'Cadence' is primarily a musical term signifying a formula of chords through the dominant to the tonic, bringing a phrase or melody or 'piece' to a satisfying close. The musical cadence may come, by analogy, to mean in language the succession of syllables which produces a similar effect. It stands to reason that there will be some accidental correspondence between the *cursus* forms and the endings of English clauses and sentences; and it is entirely reasonable to suppose that certain writers whose ear was trained to catch the *cursus* in Greek and Latin prose would sometimes naturally reproduce them in their English writing; but it cannot be proved that any English writer deliberately cultivated the *cursus* formulas in the same sense as they were cultivated by Isocrates, Cicero, and the *dictamen* practitioners.

So much is fairly simple and fairly certain. But when one sets out to look for equivalents of the *cursus* in English, one will surely find them, or rather, as some students of the subject have done, invent extensions which they pass off as equivalents. This complicates without illuminating the whole matter. Moreover, since the *cursus* and their 'equivalents' are metrical in form, there is a tendency to confuse any similar series of feet with the true *cursus* and thus nullify the real force of the true *cursus*, which is to signal a pause.

One thing, however, we can do: analyze the actual endings of English clauses and sentences to see what formulas frequently occur, i.e., discover what are the so-called native cadences in English prose. This I have undertaken tentatively for short passages ranging from the Sunday Collects and the Bible (A.V.) through Bacon and Donne to some of our contemporaries. The results are at best merely suggestive. To avoid some of the complications of my predecessors in the field I have reckoned back only two stresses and thus almost eliminated the *velox* with its secondary accent: *vinculum fregeramus*—which I have taken as *vínculum frègerámus*, in English "beautiful inspiration." The conventional notation, counting syllables back from the ultima, would make this 7-2 (instead of 7-4̸-2). Similarly the *planus*, *víncla perfrégit*, "beauty ascendant," is 5-2; the *tardus, vincla perfrégerat,* "beauty conspicuous," is 6-3. Of the nearly 3400 cadences which I tabulated, 44 per cent end with a stressed syllable; 42 per cent with a trochee; 11 per cent with a dactyl; the remaining 3 per cent with three or more unstressed syllables. The most frequent cadences (in my collection) are: 3-1, "mortal life" (539); 4-1, "quick and the dead" (437); 4-2, "Holy Spirit" (432); 5-2, "strength and protection" (425). After these follow, at some distance; 5-1, "wisdom of the just" (243); 6-2, "written for our learning" (242); 2-1, "last day" (198); 5-3 "great humility" (134); 6-3, "malice and wickedness" (133); 3-2, "great glory" (129).

These figures are obviously too limited to justify much analysis, but I think they are sufficient to point a direction. The position of the *planus,* 5-2, is worth noting (fourth place), and seems to indicate that it is a native rather than a borrowed product. (It is the dominant cadence in my sampling of Bacon's *Henry the Seventh* and also in a rather dull learned article. With its close relative 6-2 it accounts for about 20 per cent of all the cadences in my collection.) The *tardus,* 6-3, is relatively infrequent. Gibbon alone, of my samplings, favors it: he has nearly three times the average number of examples. (He leads also in 6-2.) For the sake of curiosity, here are some examples of the *velox:*

> accepted upon mine altar—Isaiah
> flowing as from a fountain—*Advancement of Learning*
> glorious resurrection—Donne
> keeping them out of mischief—Shaw
> spelling and punctuation—the learned article

These are natural enough (the others in my collection run

largely to polysyllables in -*tion*) and serve for variety, at the least.

The fact that more than one-fourth of the English cadences (again, in my small collection) correspond roughly to the medieval *cursus* can hardly signify any real borrowing from the practitioners of the *dictamen*, inasmuch as their practice was rediscovered only in the second half of the last century and cannot be said to be generally known even now. Nor is the case much better if we assume indirect influence—'aural' transmission, as Professor Croll suggests—through the Book of Common Prayer. According to my count the three favorite cadences of the Sunday Collects are 3-1, 4-1, 4-2 (all nonmedieval), comprising 60 per cent; and the medieval cadences (5-2, 6-2, 6-3, 7-3) represent only 16 per cent. The great majority of the English cadences which are also medieval are 5-2, and the Sunday Collects stand actually at the bottom of the list in number of examples of 5-2.[13] The matter of borrowing or not is, however, hardly of the first importance. What is worth knowing—if it is true—is that the commonest cadences in English prose are probably: "mortal life," "quick and the dead," "Holy Spirit," "strength and protection."

For a specimen take this from Leigh Hunt ("On Getting Up on Cold Mornings"); I italicize the possible *cursus*, using a little latitude with regard to position and expansions:

An Italian author—*Giulio Cordara*, a Jesuit—has *written a poem* upon insects, which he be*gins by insisting*, that those troublesome and abominable little animals were cre*ated for our annoyance*, and that they were certainly not in*habitants of Paradise*. We of the north may dispute this *piece of theology*; but on the other hand, it is clear as the *snow on* *the house-tops,* that Adam was not under the ne*cessity of shaving;* and that when Eve walked out of her delicious bower, she did not step upon ice three inches thick.

Something akin to the *cursus* was recently pointed out by Mr. Cecil S. Emden. By scanning the closing words of paragraphs and essays in the *Rambler,* Mr. Cecil discovered eleven "classes" of three-shress and four-stress groups, e.g.,

> shunned by the rest of mankind
> cheerful and airy companions
> pleasure of distinction and applause
> remedied by exercise and emotion
> act of liberality and tenderness
> frequently diverted by the jokes of his buffoons
> rectify their notions or enlarge their comprehensions
> begun with his pedigree, and ended with his funeral
> artifice or folly will be diligent to counterfeit
> nobody is busy to censure or detect it
> life began to languish in motionless indifference

These "metrical patterns occur only at the ends of paragraphs; and at the end of some six epigrammatic opening sentences to paragraphs, where the same kind of effect is intended"; and there are several instances where Dr. Johnson substituted metrical for nonmetrical patterns in these positions when he revised the *Rambler* essays. Mr. Emden noted also another kind of movement, longer and freer and nonmetrical, "a comprehensive design of repeated stresses in which words, and even clauses, are elements, rather than a precise pattern of a few long and short syllables."

V

Groups—Stress Groups and Others

i

BOTH SPOKEN AND WRITTEN language divides itself into larger and smaller groups, usually separated by pauses and determined by the syntactical arrangements of the words. These pauses, indicated by the conventional marks of punctuation, are not entirely reliable for our purposes; for, as has been already said, readers frequently pause when they are not conscious of doing so and on the other hand think they pause when they do not do so, and sometimes appear to pause, or not, independently of the syntactical word groups or of the punctuation.[1]

To begin with a difficult and not too admirable sentence:

I have called this principle, by which each slight variation, if useful, is preserved, by the term Natural Selection.—Darwin

Here punctuation abounds, yet in addition to the pauses which it indicates there may be for some readers a slight pause, more or less real, more or less imagined, after "which" and after "term." The first would be chiefly for acoustical reasons, the second for syntactical reasons, since there is an invisible comma or diminutive colon between "term" and "Natural"; and careful enunciation would require something like a pause after "each."[2]

Darwin's sentence falls into five parts, of 2, 3, 1, 1, 3 stresses. Note first that there is no great emphasis on "this," and what there is is shared with the first syllable of "principle." The two words thus combine to form a single distributed stress, something like what prosodists call 'hovering accent.' Note also that but for the separation in sense between "if useful" and "is preserved" the two would unite into a group of 1+1=2, and the whole sentence would yield a rhythmic alternation of 2, 3, 2, 3 stresses. It is this break in the wrong place, more than anything else, which disturbs the flow of the sentence and destroys the rhythm.

Another sentence may be more helpful.

They were in greatcoats with scarves and comforters round their necks, and hats or caps well down; and they sat mostly in dejected attitudes, bending forward, their hands resting on the handles of their sticks, some with their chins on their hands, but all gazed in one direction over the cold grey sea.

This falls into nine groups. The pauses are marked by punctuation, except for the slight one after "greatcoats," to bring out the parallelism of "with scarves . . . and hats," and one at the close, after "direction," another diminutive colon. "Well down" is again an example of distributed stress: neither "wéll down" nor "well dówn," and certainly not two stresses. Much the same is true of "round their necks": what emphasis there may be required for "round" is carried forward and absorbed with that on "necks," so that the phrase constitutes a single stress. So read, the nine groups have the following stresses: 1, 3, 3, 3 (or 4 if "sat" is emphasized), 2, 3 (or 4 if "resting" is emphasized), 3, 4, 3; and roughly speaking the length of each group measured by duration of time in reading or speaking is adequately represented by the number of stresses. The rhythm is apparent. It is plain to the ear, just as the want of it in Darwin's sentence was plain to the ear, without analysis; and the ear is supported by what the analytical examination of the sentence reveals—a series of threes and fours, not absolutely regular, but with recognizable approximation.

Two more examples analyzed minutely should be helpful.

Therefore, if thine enemy hunger, feed him; if he thirst, give him drink: for in so doing thou shalt heap coals of fire on his head.—Rom. 12: 20.

The rhetorical pattern here is A A B or strophe, antistrophe, and epode. The parallelism and balance are unmistakable, but the parts are apparently unequal. Let us see. The first member, "if thine enemy hunger, feed him," contains three stresses $(2 + 1)$, six words $(4 + 2)$, and nine syllables $(7 + 2)$; the second, "if he thirst, give him drink," three stresses $(1 + 2)$, six words $(3 + 3)$, and six syllables $(3 + 3)$; the next, "for in so doing," one (distributed) stress, four words, and five syllables; the next, "thou shalt heap," one stress, three words, three syllables; and the last, "coals of fire on his head," three stresses, six words, six syllables. The stress groups for the whole are thus 3, 3; 1, 1, 3. The threes are different in that the first is divided $2 + 1$, the second $1 + 2$, and the third is undivided, but they have the same number of words and two of them the same number of syllables. The ones are less uniform, and perhaps the latter half of the sentence should be taken as a unit of five stresses $(1 + 1 + 3)$.[3] The general proportions are therefore:

stresses	words	syllables
6 (3 + 3)	12 (6 + 6)	15 (9 + 6)
5 (1 + 1 + 3)	13 (4 + 3 + 6)	14 (5 + 3 + 6)

and the relations of stress to the other components are fairly clear.

When all is done, human life is, at the greatest and the best, but like a froward child, that must be played with and humoured a little to keep it quiet till it falls asleep, and then the care is over.

This from Temple is not more difficult than the preceding example, but more complex in appearance, the chief difference being in the conversational or informal tone, which is at the same time harmonious with the manner of expression and a foil to the idea which underlies the manner. The sentence divides itself thus:

	stresses	words	syllables
When all is done,	2	4	4
human life is,	2	3	4
at the greatest and the best,	2	6	7
but like a froward child,	2	5	6
that must be played with and humoured a little	3	9	11
to keep it quiet till it falls asleep,	4 (2 + 2)	8	10
and then the care is over	3	6	7

There is some uncertainty, at a first reading, about the false emphasis on "is," produced by the pause or suspension before the parenthesis ("at the greatest and the best"); but the two-stress grouping certainly dominates, and one sees on second reading how the lengthened or half-stressed "is" matches the half-stressed "but like" a moment later. What should be noticed is, however, that the two-stress groups do call the tune in spite of the varia-

tions among their parts. Then the tune changes to 3, 4,
3 (but with a reminiscence of the former tune in the
2 + 2), and still it is notable how the two threes, in
spite of their component differences, do actually balance
each other, the lightness of the one against the sadness,
ritardando, of the other.

ii

The assumption just indulged, that we may gauge the
rhythm, or at least one part of it, by counting stresses,
must be explained. It is something that cannot really be
proved. One may regard it provisionally as a theoretic
basis of measurement, or one may say that it commends
itself as representing more nearly and more clearly than
any other the effect immediately perceived by one's
rhythmic sense. The alternative is to measure the periods
of time between the stresses; which is certainly, according to the best theory, the only sound method, inasmuch
as rhythm consists of approximately or apparently equal
time intervals between stresses. But as a practical matter,
how measure these periods of time? One may tap them
off, as Thomson does, and record the fractions, or as
Patterson does, with musical notation; but these methods are cumbersome, and the result is of doubtful value
because the very act of tapping sets up an artificial or
self-conscious attitude which must go far towards vitiating
accuracy. It destroys the natural movement and offers
a deliberately studied substitute. It has the air of accuracy
without its virtue of truth. The other way is the accuracy
of mechanical recordings, the laboratory method. But
even this yields not the true temporal values of phrase
or sentence, but the actual periods of time occupied in
the reading by one or more experimenters. The average

of many recordings made by well-chosen readers will certainly give us a valuable approximation and is, if properly understood, by no means to be flouted. It is scientific. But its deceptive appearance of objective accuracy is a danger not to be overlooked or underestimated.

So, between Scylla and Charybdis there is never safety. Neither the laboratory record nor the subjective report is absolutely trustworthy. When the one corroborates the other, we may feel fairly safe; for the rest we must admit our uncertainty and try to make the best of it.[4] A fair compromise seems to be counting the stresses and assuming that this gives us a reasonable indication of the duration of the group. It is a concession to weakness, or to convenience, or to both. Not all two-stress groups are of the same length, nor are all three-stress groups of the same length; they do not need to be in order to testify to their rhythmic value. Since duration is the important factor, we may regard the stresses as its coefficient: therefore when we speak of a group of so many stresses, we mean a group of such a duration. The stresses serve as a measure of time, and we might well enough speak of a two-unit group or a three-unit group meaning by unit a relative division of time which is marked off by the stress and the unstressed elements associated with it.[5]

This principle announced, it remains now to examine its various forms and study its various movements.[6]

One of the commonest varieties is a binary grouping, so prevalent in some writers as to constitute almost a rhythmic habit, satisfying no doubt something deep-rooted in their subconscious. Its danger is of course monotony. It would be interesting to know to what extent they actually are conscious of it and to what extent it is inherent in the language.[7] It is fairly regular in Gibbon, as in this fragment from chapter xxii of the *Decline and Fall:*

When we inspect with minute, | or perhaps malevolent, | attention | the portrait of Julian, | something seems wanting | to the grace and perfection | of the whole figure. |His genius was | less powerful and sublime | than that of Caesar, | nor did he possess | the consummate prudence | of Augustus. The virtue of Trajan | appears more steady and natural, | and the philosophy of Marcus | is more simple and consistent. | Yet Julian sustained | adversity with firmness, | and prosperity with moderation. | After an interval of one hundred and twenty years from the death of Alexander Severus, the Romans beheld an emperour | who made no distinction | between his duties and his pleasures, | who laboured | to relieve the distress | and to revive the spirit | of his subjects, | and who endeavoured always | to connect authority with merit, | and happiness with virtue. | Even faction, | and religious faction, | was constrained to acknowledge | the superiority of his genius | in peace as well as in war, | and to confess, with a sigh, | that the apostate Julian | was a lover of his country, | and that he deserved | the empire of the world.

Some of the divisions may be disputable, but not enough to upset the count seriously; and two-thirds of them contain two stresses. The movement of the passage is therefore unmistakable: along with the syntactic balance and parallelism there is a "stately and consistent" two-stress rhythmical unit.

Take three more passages, almost at random from entirely different kinds of writers, one from *The Last Chronicle of Barset,* the second from *The Stones of Venice,* the third from an academic committee report. All three, Trollope, Ruskin, and the professor, exhibit the same tendency.

On the morning of the Sunday | after the dean's return | Mr. Harding was lying in his bed, | and Posy was sitting | on the bed beside him.| It was manifest to all now | that he became | feebler and feebler | from day to day, | and that he would never leave | his bed again.| Even the archdeacon | had shaken his head, | and had acknowledged to his wife | that the last day | for her father was near at hand. | It would soon be necessary | that he should select | another vicar | for St. Ewolds.

We find ourselves | in a paved alley, | some seven feet wide | where it is widest, | full of people, | and resonant with cries | of itinerant salesmen,— | a shriek in their beginning, | and dying away | into a kind of brazen ringing, | all the worse for its confinement | between the high houses | of the passage along which | we have to make our way. Overhead | an inextricable confusion | of rugged shutters, | and iron balconies | and chimney flues | pushed out on brackets | to save room, | and arched windows | with projecting sills | of Istrian stone, | and gleams of green leaves | here and there | where a fig-tree branch | escapes over a lower wall | from some inner cortile, | leading the eye up | to the narrow stream | of blue sky | high over all.

"The University Review," for October | contains an interesting discussion | of This Research Business | from the humanistic standpoint | by a Commission of the Association | which visited selected institutions. | The Association is planning | to send a similar Commission | to the United States | in 1933, | if details can be arranged, | and hopes to have at least informal contacts of interest with representatives | of our American Association. | While problems of academic freedom and tenure appear to be | far less acute and abundant | than in the United States, | it is noted that | a situation of this kind | has recently arisen | in the University of Durham | College of Medicine | and has been the subject | of formal action | on the part of the Association.

The bars, needless to say, are for expository emphasis merely. They do not always indicate real pauses nor always logical subdivisions, but sometimes almost imperceptible divisions themselves created by the binary rhythms already apparent.

A good illustration of how these binary groups can even dominate the others with which they appear is this sentence from Bacon's "Of Truth":

Surely the *wickedness of falsehood* and *breach of faith* cannot possibly be so *highly expressed*, as in that it shall be the *last peal* to call the *judgments of God* upon the *generations of men*: it being foretold that, when *Christ cometh*, he shall not find *faith upon earth*.

I have italicized the twos to show how by repetition they gain such emphasis as to reduce the longer groups to their own pattern.

iv

The human propensity to run adjectives in threes is well known, and the deep-seated preference for triads of all kinds; but one finds few examples so conspicuous for three-stress groupings. Here are two, however.

In the firm expectation that | when London shall be a habitation of bitterns, | when St. Paul and Westminster Abbey | shall stand shapeless and nameless ruins | in the midst of an unpeopled marsh, | when the piers of Waterloo Bridge | shall become the nuclei | of islets of reeds and osiers, | and cast the jagged shadows | of their broken arches on the solitary stream, some Transatlantic commentator will be weighing in the scales of some new and unimagined system of criticism the respective merits of the Bells and the Fudges and their historians.—Shelley, Dedication to "Peter Bell the Third."

Deprived of | that prodigious nourishment of the shop | in

the fashionable seaport of Helmstone, | he retired upon his
native town, | the Cinque Port of Crikswich, | where he
rented the cheapest residence | he could discover for habita-
tion, | the House on the Beach, and lived imposingly, though
not in total disaccord | with his old mother's principles.—
Meredith, *The House on the Beach.*

Usually the two-stress group predominates, with three-
stress groups for variation—as in Bacon's "Certainly, it
is a heaven upon earth, to have a man's mind move in
charity, rest in providence, and turn upon the poles of
truth"—all groups of two until the last, which is particularly welcome after the repeated *cursus planus.* In
this sentence from Raleigh's *History of the World* the
twos predominate by a ratio of eight to five:

They themselves would rather have wished to have stolen
out of the world without noise, than to be put in mind that
they have purchased the report of their actions in the world,
by rapine, oppression, and cruelty, by giving in spoil the
innocent and labouring soul to the idle and insolent, and
by having emptied the cities of the world of their ancient
inhabitants, and filled them again with so many and so
variable sorts of sorrows.

In this from DeQuincey, which Saintsbury denominates
"a perfect type in miniature of rhythmed prose,"[8] the
twos and threes are cunningly mingled. Note the gradation: one, two, three (if a stress be allowed on "neither,"
as it probably should be in consideration of the tone and
tempo of the whole sentence); then the three between the
semicolons; then the long close made up of two twos and
a three, to say nothing of the metrical undertones and
the final *cursus tardus.*

And her eyes if they were ever seen would be neither sweet
nor subtle; no man could read their story; they would be

found filled with perishing dreams and the wrecks of for-gotten delirium.

Bacon again gives us a fine example in which the run of twos in the beginning, each in itself very different, rises to a sort of climax with two threes, followed by a two which is like the subsidence of a wave, with a spondaic fall. The great chancellor, who apparently had no cul-tivated ear for music, had assuredly a most delicate sense of the sound of prose.

But little do men perceive what solitude is, and how far it extendeth. For a crowd is not company; and faces are but a gallery of pictures; and talk but a tinkling cymbal, where there is no love.—"Of Friendship."

Finally, here is a specimen of unstudied threes from a popular columnist (1947):

> As indicated in previous reports,
> American abandonment of Italy
> in her present economic plight
> will almost certainly bring in
> a Communist dominated government
>   in the Spring.

v

In the previous examples the groups have been al-most all of two and three stresses; longer groups, of four and five stresses, occasionally occur, as in the fol-lowing specimen from DeQuincey.

> Out of the darkness,
>   if I happen to call back the image of Fanny,
> uprises suddenly
>   from a gulf of forty years
> a rose in June;
>   or if I think for a moment of the rose in June,
>   uprises the heavenly face of Fanny.

> One after the other,
>   like the antiphonies in the choral service,
>   rise Fanny and the rose in June;
> then, back again,
>   the rose in June and Fanny.
> Then come both together, as in a chorus,
>   roses and Fannies,
>   Fannies and Roses,
>   without end,
>   thick as blossoms in Paradise.

This is of course a studio piece, the most deliberate kind of poetic prose; though the metrical element is carefully subdued, there is at least one blank verse line; and I have ventured to print it as free verse. But what should be especially noticed is the larger groupings, transcending slight pauses and even marks of punctuation in the smaller sections, and in the longer sections according to semicolons and full stops. To the first bar there are thirteen stresses, to the next eight, to the next thirteen again, and in the last section twelve. Within the longer rhythms the divisions are equally interesting: in the first, a rise and fall—2, 4, 2, 3, 2; in the second, 4, 4—an even balance; in the third, a series of twos and threes; in the last, three fours divided 3+1, 2+2, 1+3. These statistical details—no one would dream that DeQuincey computed them in advance—may help to reveal what the ear perceives more vaguely; and they may be forgotten when the passage is read over again.

There are some interesting groupings in this from Trollope's *Autobiography:*

That some facts were stated inaccurately, I do not doubt;	3 + 2
that many opinions were crude, I am quite sure;	3 + 2
that I failed to understand much which I attempted	

to explain, is possible. $5(2 + 3) + 1$
But with all these faults the book was a thoroughly
                              honest book $2 + 4$
and was the result of unflagging labour for a
                     period of fifteen months. $3 + 3$

The arrangements of this famous sentence of Arnold's
are perhaps a bit too obvious, but are characteristic of his
quasi-oratorical style:

And yet,
   steeped in sentiment as she lies,   3
   spreading her garments to the moonlight,   3
   and whispering from her towers the last enchant-
          ment of the middle ages, $2 + 3$
   who will deny that Oxford   3
     by her ineffable charm,   2
   keeps ever calling us nearer to the true goal of
          all of us, $3 + 3$
     to the ideal, to perfection,—to beauty,
          in a word, $3(+1)$
   which is truth seen from another side—   4
   nearer, perhaps, than all the science of Tübingen.   5

vi

I shall now examine in some detail one of the finest
examples of all English rhythmical prose, a passage
"than which," said Saintsbury, "I hardly know anything
more exquisitely rhythmed in the whole range of English from Ælfric to Pater."[9]

If some king of the earth have so large an extent of domain
in north and south, as that he hath winter and summer together in his dominions; so large an extent east and west
as that he hath day and night together in his dominions,
much more hath God mercy and justice together. He
brought light out of darkness, not out of lesser light; He
can bring thy summer out of winter, though thou have no
spring; though in the ways of fortune, or understanding,

or conscience thou have been benighted till now, wintered
and frozen, clouded and eclipsed, damped and benumbed,
smothered and stupefied till now, now God comes to thee,
not as in the dawning of the day, not as in the bud of the
spring, but as the sun at noon, to illustrate all shadows, as
the sheaves in harvest, to fill all penuries. All occasions in-
vite His mercies, and all times are His seasons.—Donne,
XXX Sermons, Sermon II.

The balance and parallelisms throughout the two long
sentences need no pointer: they are however important
sources of the rhythmical effect. In the first sentence and
the beginning of the second they are so regular as to be
almost stanzaic:

> If some king of the earth
>   have so large an extent of dominion
>   in north and south
>   as that he hath winter and summer
>   together in his dominions;
>   so large an extent
>   east and west
>   as that he hath day and night
>   together in his dominions,
>   much more hath God
>   mercy and justice together.

Here the protasis rises in a long curve, which is repeated
in an almost exactly parallel curve, and the three-stress
group at the start is balanced by the three-stress groups at
the close. The two curves, each of four lines, are made
up of two-stress groups (varying from three to ten syllables), with one exception: the first has three beats instead of two, agreeing with the first line and avoiding the
repetition of "dominions" after the second "so large an
extent"; and this is compensated by the curtailing of the
refrain to "together" at the end. Or, if read slowly, the

fourth and eighth lines may be taken as four-stress: "as
thàt he háth"—which adds to the variety and complexity.

The second sentence begins with a simple quatrain,
with a subordinate trochaic movement in the third line:
"bring thy summer out of winter."

> He brought light out of darkness,
>   not out of lesser light;
> He can bring thy summer out of winter,
>   though thou have no spring.

But the wave which seems to have subsided with the
quatrain rises on a new "though"-clause to the repeated
"till now"—

> though in the ways of fortune, or understanding,
>   or conscience
> thou have been benighted till now,
>   wintered and frozen,
>   clouded and eclipsed,
>   damped and benumbed,
>   smothered and stupefied till now—

culminating with the three adjacent stresses of "now God
comes," and subsides, undulating, to the stanzaic alternation of two- and three-beat lines—

> not as in the dawning of the day,
> not as in the bud of the spring,
>   but as the sun at noon,
>   to illustrate all shadows,
>   as the sheaves in harvest,
>   to fill all penuries.

The third sentence is a coda, complete with a *cursus* to
match that of the first sentence—

> All occasions invite His mercies
>   and all times are His seasons.

This exploring of the mechanism, it may be asked—
how much does it reveal of the rhythm itself? The answer depends: for those who have an inquiring turn of
mind and those who are fascinated by machinery, the answer is simple. For those who are distressed by any
minute examination of detail, the negative answer is
equally simple; for them nothing can be explained, nothing that has to do with the mysteries of the arts. They
must apprehend everything directly, intuitively, or not
at all; and they are often to be envied. But if one is to
try to explain, if one is to reach below the apparent and
look for the 'hidden springs,' one must try all the methods. And for the still unconvinced, here is a specimen
from Pater, who is our modern representative of numerous prose. His effects and his means may be sometimes
too obvious for good art, but they are the more suited to
exposition.

For the essence of humanism	2
is that one belief[10]	2
of which he seems never to have doubted,	2
that nothing which has ever interested	3
living men and women	3
can wholly lose its vitality—	3
no language they have spoken,	3
nor oracle beside which they have hushed their voices,	4
no dream which has once been entertained	4
by actual human minds,	3
nothing about which they have ever been passionate,	4
or expended time and zeal.	3

Note on Isochronism

So much is made by some theorists of the necessity
of equal intervals of time if the rhythm is to be true
rhythm that it seems worth while to include here the re-

sults of the only thoroughgoing attempt I know to investigate the problem, *The Rhythm of English Prose*,
by André Classe. Those results are very restricted, partly
by the author's severely scientific cautiousness and partly
by the limitations of his experiments with the kymograph, but they are, from the point of view of mechanical
measurement, the best that we have, and their value as
a check on subjective impressions must be recognized.

"Only groups of two, three, and at the most, four
syllables, form easily recognizable patterns" (p. 131).
In larger groups the same differences of quantity may be
felt, but there is then a tendency to "a levelling of the
quantity of the component syllables." Thus everything
that Mr. Classe says must be understood as referring to
these small units and not to the longer rhythmic movements. The experimental method, he has to admit (p.
91), is impractical with long passages.

Three main elements, he says (p. 89) make or mar
the rhythm of an English sentence: "The phonetic factor
of number of units in the bar," i.e., of syllables in the
group; "The logical factor of grammatical connexion
between the bars"; and "The phonetic factor of the nature of the units in the bar, especially accents," but also
the qualities of vowel and consonant. But "Although
isochronism is probably the essential characteristic of the
rhythm of English prose, it is equally certain that perfect
isochronism can only be realized when very definite conditions are fulfilled. These are: *(a)* Similarity of phonetic structure of the groups, including number of syllables. *(b)* Similarity of grammatical structure of the
groups, and similarity of connexion between the groups"
(p. 100). It stands to reason that these conditions "are
comparatively seldom met with in ordinary speech" and

in the ordinary kinds of prose. In such and "even in careful prose, we seldom feel that the accents return at *rigor-
ously* isochronous intervals. It is highly probable, of
course, that we do tend to equalize the groups we perceive and to minimize the differences. On the other
hand, it is not less likely that we tend to place the stresses
so as to facilitate the perception of groups as equal
groups" (p. 51). Twice he compares the organization of
rhythmic units to walking. "The length of the step is
largely subordinated to the various obstacles constituted
by sense and the phonetic elements, which can be compared to the irregularities of the ground. The rhythmical
speaker adapts himself more readily to the uneven going
and preserves a greater regularity of gait under difficult
conditions. The rhythmic writer makes the road even by
symmetrical spacing of the pauses and stresses" (p. 89).

Mr. Classe's most conservative statement of the case
is: "There seems to be good evidence that it [isochro-
nism] can be accepted, with some qualifications, as a characteristic which always seems to be present and to make its
influence felt; although, frequently, it only remains as an
underlying tendency of which some other factor at times
almost completely obliterates the effects" (p. 90). Or,
with even more caution: "isochronism often means nothing more than a sort of ideal which may be frequently
realized, but more often is not, especially when the
rhythmic tendency has to contend with other factors
which obscure its effects. . . . When isochronism is incompatible with logical or phonetic necessity, it must
give way before them and disappear more or less completely" (p. 87).

These reservations may seem almost completely nugatory, but they are not so intended. Their effect, however, is to heighten the emphasis on psychological and even 'elastic' time. By rigorous mechanical measurement isochronism hardly exists except by accident or under the rarest of circumstances; and if rhythm is determined solely by this criterion, rhythm itself hardly exists in prose. We must, therefore, either reject prose rhythm altogether or else modify our definition, i.e., substitute other criteria. Which is of course what all but the most hidebound purists have done. Mr. Classe began by saying: "So far as the present work is concerned, what matters is that there is a tendency to organize events in rhythmic series, that we are conscious of the existence of rhythm, and that we perceive it in speech" (p. 1). And it remains true (1) that writers—some more than others, to be sure—have always composed with attention to the sound of their sentences, in the interests of both economy and pleasure; and (2) that readers, or listeners, have always according to their capacity tried to meet them halfway or better by assisting in the organization of inequalities into semblance of equality. Strict isochronism is an ideal; our object should be to study how, and how successfully, our writers have approached the ideal.

Style — Rhythmic Effects

i

PROUST . . . has both chosen his materials with
economy and built with them monumentally,"
writes Mr. Edmund Wilson in *Axel's Castle*. The two
"with" phrases are parallel in form but not parallel in
sense. The *m* alliteration draws attention to elements
which you would expect to be parallel but are not. Thus
there are two little tunes which are out of harmony with
the sense.

"Then, suddenly, she was clinging to him, and his
arms went about her," writes Mr. Sax Rohmer, in *Em-
peror of America*. The two actions, which you would expect to find in parallel construction, since they are *simultaneous*, are presented in different tenses, or aspects; and
as in the sentence just quoted from Mr. Wilson, the conflict between form and meaning rather goes beyond the
'slight novelty' which is one of the happy characteristics
of good prose.

Whether one admire or disapprove, the effect is
plain: where you expected rhythm—similar ideas in similar form—you found something different.

"The days are short but the afternoons are long,"
says the proverb. Add a word, which changes the tune
ever so slightly, and the emphasis is increased greatly:
—"The days are short but the afternoons are very long"
—for the added word not only strengthens the contrast

between the short first clause and the appropriately longer second one, but it also sets up a metrical run of four iambs which slow down the whole delivery. In the first version "afternoons" has one stress, in the second it has almost two.

"It is a dangerous cruel river, as cruel as it is beautiful, and the hill people say it has to take a life a year," writes Miss Rumer Godden in *Thus Far and No Farther.* Try it this way: "It is a cruel river, as cruel as it is beautiful." The swiftness is diminished, but with the concentration on "cruel" the contrast with "beautiful" is increased, and this contrast lays a slight (at least) emphasis on the second "is."

In such, as in many other small ways, do rhythm and style play a continual counterpoint.

"We ran past them faster than ever mill-race in our inexorable flight," wrote DeQuincy in *The English Mail Coach;* but when he revised the sentence for the Collected Works he made a chiastic change: "Faster than ever mill-race we ran past them in our inexorable flight." The second form is certainly better on rhetorical grounds because it brings the two most emphatic elements at the beginning and end of the sentence. And the separation of "ran past" and "faster than" is equally an improvement. But can one say more? The idea is one of rapidity; and both versions end with the two long anapests. The difference is in the 'attack.' The first version begins without a suggestion of speed: "ran" and "past" have almost equal emphasis, and the syllables do not accelerate until the fifth word. In the second version however the tempo is rapid from the outset, and with the gathered speed comes a subordination of "ran": so that only the semi-spondaic "mill-race" retards the movement, and instead of the former grouping of 2-3-2 there is a 3-3 (dividing with the slight pause after "-race") in which the second three has twelve syllables against seven of the first.

Anyone recognizes, even when he does not explain it to himself, a difference between the conventional "The night fell dark and chilly" and the 'modern' way of saying it (which has been condemned as spasmodic): "The night fell dark, chilly." The one is smooth and the other abrupt; it is not that one is good and the other reprehensible, but that they *are* different and either may be right in its place.

ii

The word 'style' is commonly used in two very different senses which are often merged and confused. In the one sense style is the skilful or successful use of the mechanical elements of language—the sound and meaning of words, their forms and syntactical arrangement. The writer of a 'correct style' (a somewhat damning and old-fashioned phrase) manages these elements according to the rules; the master of an 'easy style' handles them without apparent effort; the practitioner of a 'poetic style' adorns them with beauties of his own adding; and so on. Or, to go a little further, style is something to be achieved. By playing the sedulous ape to the classics, where style is known to abound, the writer learns, like an actor, to say a thing which is not his own in a way which is not his own and therefore presumably better than he could manage unaided. This might be called the composite or negative style. At its best, however, it is what we call a command of the resources of language.

The other sense of the word 'style' is what causes our difficulty: it is somewhat metaphysical and 'mystical.'

It stands forth in the familiar *mot*: the style is the man
—Buffon. A man writes naturally, thus expressing both
himself and what he has to communicate. We hear his
voice, as Mr. Dobrée says. But there is a kind of fallacy
here, for in the state of civilization which we now pro-
fess it is doubtful if we do anything naturally. The *man
himself* is a bundle of affectations and acquirements, of
ways and means which are *not himself*, but what he regards as most necessary or suitable to produce his effect on
his audience. For even the symbolists do not write *in
vacuo*.

One escape from this circle is the variation of Remy
de Gourmont: "Le signe de l'homme dans l'œuvre intel-
lectuelle, c'est la pensée. La pensée est l'homme même.
Le style est la pensée même." That is, style is the special
manner of writing which is peculiar to both the writer
and his subject. No one else would say just that thing in
just that way. The garment should fit the body, but
there must be a body to wear it. In this sense the test
and measure of a style is a composite of intention and
content, and the distinctions of plain and colored, conversational and ornate, with their extremes of pedestrian
and purple, are but functions of the two elements, useful
for descriptive purposes but hardly illuminating for
analysis. And similarly there is a host of adjectives—
denominative but not analytical—to describe the effects
of this or that style: slow and swift, staccato or jerky
and smooth or undulant, dulcet and noisy, jog-trot
and soaring, formal and flamboyant, uninvolved and
intrinsicate.

In any case, however, the present concern is not style
in general but the role of rhythm in any or all of these
various *styles*.

It goes without saying that for success in communication between writer and reader all the arts and crafts of language are less than enough; for when all has been done which the writer can do, the reader may still be ill prepared or so perverse as to miss the effect. But at the very least the clothing *should* fit the body. If a bit of pedestrian research is presented in the manner of a popular lecture or if a pathetic incident is related in the language of our daily press, the incongruity is shocking. And there are less obvious instances, as when Ruskin expounds his views of Gothic sculpture in the language of rhapsody or undertakes to teach mineralogy as though it were poetry. A more impressive illustration is Milton's "Areopagitica," an earnest, reasoned argument for the repeal of a parliamentary measure. Everyone praises the "Areopagitica" as a masterpiece of English prose, yet many have felt something to be wrong and probably many will accept Mr. Middleton Murry's admission: whenever he reads it, he says, "the last thing I find myself thinking about . . . is the liberty of unlicensed printing. It might much rather be a poem on the immortality of the human soul" (p. 124).

The reason, in Mr. Murry's opinion, for this discrepancy between Milton's purpose and his effect on the reader is a matter of rhythm.[1] He finds the work irresistible—although the "governors of the Commonwealth" then did not—but "the superb music is too dominant." Is this a serious charge? Mr. Murry states the case from another point of view, that of the writer, in an earlier passage in the same essay ("The Problem of Style").

It is so easy to allow the sound of a phrase to overpower the sense, even when the sense is fairly clear; for when a strong, decided rhythmical movement is running in one's head, it is very hard not to submit to its influence, and blunt the edge of one's phrase by continually replacing the less by the more sonorous word. . . . When the musical suggestion is allowed to predominate, decadence of style has begun.

And even more severely he adds:

The writer who allows himself to be distracted by the musical possibilities of language is like the dog who dropped the bone for the watery shadow. (p. 86)

It is a charge, this of sacrificing the substance for the shadow, which few writers altogether escape, and it is fundamental in any view of the relation of style and rhythm. But as there are times when he who would save his soul may run the risk of losing it, so there are times when the shadow may be more than mere substance. Perhaps Mr. Murry would admit, if pressed, that it is not alone the dominant music which renders the "Areopagitica" more like a poem on the immortality of the soul than an argument against the imprimatur. Milton certainly knew that he was pleading for freedom of thought and speech and that his zeal in this plea was carrying him beyond his immediate goal. In this sense, then, the energy of his "music" was justified in so far as the "Areopagitica" remains one of the finest appeals ever written for toleration and truth. As the garment expanded, the body grew to more than life size.

It is perhaps worth a note in passing to see Mr. Murry trespass, in miniature, on the same ground. Says he, on page 10 of the same essay: "They will enjoy a languid sequence of *succès d'estime* in their lives and be quietly forgotten after their deaths." The rhythmic balance of *in their lives* and *after their deaths* is a false note. The first part of the sentence is properly longer than the second, and the approach to meter carries a suggestion of scorn for those who favor the flat style and who hold that to be vivid is to be vulgar. But if the second part were still shorter, if he had said ". . . and then be quietly forgotten" instead of pursuing the too obvious parallelism, the curve would have been right: a rapid falling cadence, a quick forgetting.

Illustrations are to be found everywhere, for we all compose partly 'by ear' and the ear often betrays us. So: "The women in their red cloaks and straw hats, the elder children with bare heads and bare feet. . ." —Scott, *Guy Mannering*. Does the second "bare" serve any purpose but balance? Perhaps more can be said for the repetition in Stevenson's "considered us in the light of creatures brutally strong and brutally silly." How does one understand Shelley's "It is the perfect and consummate surface and bloom of all things"? Are the two adjectives a kind of compound modifying both nouns? or are they distributed in direct or chiastic order? or is the doubling only a balance for its own sake? Compare Landor's ". . . my father, sitting in the coolest part of the house, exchanged his last measure of grain for a chlamys of scarlet cloth fringed with silver." The "last measure of grain" and "chlamys of scarlet cloth" have a very pretty asymmetrical balance, but "scarlet chlamys" would be simpler. Or note, on the other hand, how avoidance of parallel construction may violate both grammar and rhythm, as in Mr. Maugham's "When he smiled you saw that he had exquisite teeth. They were very white, small and of a perfect shape." Did Mr. Maugham think that "white, small, and perfect in shape" would be monotonous? or "white, small, and in shape perfect" too emphatic?

So in large and in small, the influence of rhythm is

pervasive: it may determine the form of expression for better or for worse. And often one cannot be sure, even in one's own writing, how strong the influence is; still less in analyzing what others have written. For there are not only the moments of inattention, but also moments, and longer periods, when thought and expression remain in solution; and even after the sentence is precipitated in words there may, or may not, follow the periods of revision. Sometimes the words seem to flow without uncertainty and without conflict between the demands of grammar and the requirements of expressiveness; but even then who knows what prepared curves and acquired collocations have set the pattern in the subconscious mind?

iii

There is nothing remarkable in the rhythm of this sentence:

To most people Mr. Grobe's behaviour was both gentle and loving, and he had lived the same pure life for twenty years.

It has an easy equable movement which follows the simple meaning it conveys. But in its original form—I have changed three words without altering its apparent rhythm—the effect is different because the sense is different. The tune is not gentle, but waspish. There is a sarcastic curl to the identical curve:

To most people Mr. Grobe's behaviour was both gentle and loving, and he had worn the same black tie for twenty years.[2]

This is curious, and seems to mean, unless one is the victim of one's imagination, that the same rhythm can produce opposite effects or that there is no inherent significance in a rhythm independent of the thing expressed.

On the other hand, to take another example from Mr. Powys, there is a fittingness in the broken movement at the close of the following sentence, after the comparative smoothness of the first part, which is certainly unambiguous and could hardly go with any other idea. "He" is St. Paul.

There are passages, indeed, in his writings where his trust in his crucified Prometheus mounts up to such an ecstasy of victory that the dark horrors of that ultimate arbitrary will are swept away, and a huge wave of universal reconciliation tosses up the very silt of the abyss into the light, and *Christ with the whole creation in his heart* loses Himself in the cosmic mystery into which he is diffused; till "God"—but a very different "God" from the one who "has mercy on whom he will have mercy and hardeneth whom he will harden," and a still more different "God" from the Johannine Love-Circle floating on the black waters of the Abyss—"becomes all in all."

In a lecture on "Modern Prose Style," afterwards included in his book of the same title, Mr. Bonamy Dobrée suggested that the distinguishing mark of modern English prose in contrast to the earlier styles is largely its conversational tone. Comparing a passage from Sir Thomas Browne and one from William James, he found that "It is pretty obvious that the difference lies in the rhythm." Then, admitting that "that is too easy a thing to say," he goes on: "and as a matter of fact, if we analyze these two passages into 'prose rhythms' in the way that Saintsbury did in his fascinating book, they are not, prosodically speaking at least, so different after all" (p. 213). This may be a judgment on Saintsbury's method or on Mr. Dobrée's method. Let us see.

The first passage is from Browne's *Christian Morals,*

the second from James's *The Will to Believe.* To these
let us add one from Adam Smith (from Saintsbury, pp.
263 ff.), one taken at random from Dryden's *Of Dramatic Poesy,* and one taken at random from Mr. Dobrée
himself (p. 221).[3] I have spaced them to indicate the
proportions of the members, and added some statistical
details for what they may be worth.

Let thy studies be free as thy thoughts and contemplations:
but fly not upon the wings of imagination;
join sense unto reason, and experiment unto speculation,
and so give life unto embryon truths
and verities yet in their chaos.
There is nothing more acceptable unto the ingenious world,
than this noble eluctation of truth;
wherein, against the tenacity of prejudice and prescription,
this century now prevaileth.

On the whole, then,
we must conclude that no philosophy of ethics is possible
in the old-fashioned absolute sense of the term.
Everywhere the ethical philosopher must wait on facts.
The thinkers who create the ideals come he knows not
    whence,
their sensibilities are evolved he knows not how;
and the question as to which of two conflicting ideals will
    give the best universe then and there,
can be answered by him only through the aid of the experi-
    ence of other men.

The violator of the more sacred laws of justice
can never reflect on the sentiments
which mankind must entertain with regard to him,
without feeling all the agonies of shame and horror and
    consternation.
When his passion is gratified,
and he begins coolly to reflect on his past conduct,
he can enter into none of the motives which influenced it.

They appear now as detestable to him
as they did always to other people.

Another thing in which the French differ from us and
     from the Spaniards,
is, that they do not embarrass, or cumber themselves with
     too much plot;
they only represent so much of a story
as will constitute one whole and great action sufficient for
     a play:
we, who undertake more, do but multiply adventures;
which, not being produced from one another,
as effects from causes,
but barely following,
constitute many actions in the drama,
and consequently make it many plays.

It is not so simple as it sounds
for a man to watch his own mind;
it is as difficult as writing in the way you ordinarily talk:
literary habits continually get in the way.
Nor must a man write as he might lazily talk,
and it is more important than ever for him
to reject the dead metaphor
which can never be more than an approximation,
to choose the exact, the expressive word,
to rid his style of fat,
to make it athletic.

	No. of words	No. of monosyllables	% of monosyllables	No. of syllables	Stressed syllables	% of unstressed syllables
Browne	67	39	58	116	34	71
James	83	60	72	122	39	68
Smith	73	45	61.6	114	34	70
Dryden	79	52	63	121	41	66
Dobrée	84	67	77	116	37	68

The most striking variation here is the larger percentage
of monosyllabic words in James and Mr. Dobrée—a very

likely characteristic of modern style. But on the other hand the proportion of stressed to unstressed syllables which should be an index of tempo, is slightly in Browne's favor. The rhythmic units are in fact longer in the James passage than in the Browne passage. It may well be that what makes Sir Thomas Browne seem old-fashioned and William James modern is the vocabulary, the "thy" and "-eth," as against the colloquial "On the whole, then" (in spite of the archaic "he knows not how"), rather than the rhythm. To me, at any rate, the Dryden passage sounds as modern as Mr. Dobrée's sentences.

Now, to make the confusion a little worse, consider five more passages, of mixed chronology. The first is from a contemporary, but is as balanced (perhaps for ironic effect) as though it came from the eighteenth century. The second *is* from the eighteenth century, yet has a smooth continuous flow without any obvious tricks; the plain narrative style, at home in any century. The third is again contemporary, slightly mannered but unmistakably modern. The fourth is a specimen of the ultramodern in briskness verging on flippancy. The fifth is from a book written in the most persistently conversational and informal style. There can hardly be a question of any conscious stylistic aim beyond that of being agreeably enthusiastic. Yet note the rhythmic balance and the metrical runs, which afford little preparation for the flat a-rhythm of the last sentence. "On the whole, then," if rhythm is a clue to modernity, it is difficult to distinguish as such.

The armies [of the benighted] are full of pleasant and pious folk. But they have yielded to the only enemy that matters—the enemy within. They have sinned against passion and truth, and vain will be their strife after virtue.

As the years pass, they are censured. Their pleasantry and their piety show cracks, their wit becomes cynicism, their unselfishness hypocrisy; they fall and produce discomfort wherever they go. They have sinned against Eros and against Pallas Athene, and not by any heavenly intervention, but by the ordinary course of nature, those allied deities will be avenged.—E. M. Forster.

The number of people increased, and in less than half an hour the island was moved and raised in such a manner, that the lowest gallery appeared in a parallel of less than a hundred yards distance from the height where I stood. I then put myself into the most supplicating postures, and spoke in the humblest accent, but received no answer. Those who stood nearest over against me seemed to be persons of distinction, as I supposed by their habit. They conferred earnestly with each other, looking often upon me. At length one of them called out in a clear, polite, smooth dialect, not unlike in sound to the Italian; and therefore I returned an answer in that language, hoping at least that the cadence might be more agreeable to his ears. Although neither of us understood the other, yet my meaning was easily known, for the people saw the distress I was in.—Jonathan Swift.

One of the great social changes in the nineties was the sudden use of the bicycle among the leisured. The bicycle had been there for a long time, first as the velocipede, an enormous high contraption, one huge wheel and a little wheel; then as the bone-shaker, without tyres; then as the "safety bicycle," with india-rubber tyres. But nobody dared ride it; not from physical fear, but because it was not the thing. When I was at Cambridge it was as little the thing as anything could be. It was as bad as wearing a billycock hat and a frock coat. Then suddenly, in the summer of 1894, I think, it began to be the thing, and people bicycled just for the fun of bicycling anywhere, even indoors if they could not bicycle out of doors, and there were bicycling breakfast-parties in Battersea Park; somebody once had a bicycle that could go uphill. It was called le rêve, and it was but a dream, and it was broken.—Maurice Baring.

John was in his thirties, but he had not changed, Margaret disliked the idea of his going to Edinburgh to lecture. He was not 'quite ready,' she said, to stand up on a platform before ordinary men. Knowing him as she did, she was secretly amazed that he should think he was; for as he appeared to her he was still a delicate child needing to be nursed by herself and Effie. John was an artist at creating traffic without movement, as he had done on the carpet at Brunswick Square, and he sat beside a toy still, in rapt amusement. Like a child's, too, was his benevolent contempt for people. He lifted them up for a moment's inspection and deposited them on the ground in hopeless remoteness. He was impartial after the manner of children, to all except the one or two kind souls who mothered him. For these he had a special smile. It was his secret grievance that Effie had never really sought to gain his affection in this way. She received from him the same bland welcome as the baker's boy. But he kept his promise that he would introduce her to his interesting friends the more easily as he had Effie's love of people, not so much for themselves as because they made eddies through which his soul could vibrate long before it came to the outer fringe of solitude. He put his money down and had his houseful. They were at hand when he wanted them for a luncheon or a sunset; and when he did not want them, he glided gently towards the door and left them to Effie.—David Larg, *John Ruskin*.

The average gardener, in the cold dark days of December and January, sits by his fire, turning over the pages of seed catalogues, wondering what he shall sow for the spring. If he goes out in his garden at all, it is only for the sake of exercise. He puts on a coat, stamps up and down the frozen paths, hardly deigns to glance at the black, empty beds, turns in again. Perhaps, before returning to his fireside, he may go and look into a dark cupboard to see if the hyacinths, in fibre, are beginning to sprout. But that represents the sum total of his activity.—Beverley Nichols, *Down the Garden Path*.

iv

Follow now some small specimens which are curious
—perhaps in both senses of the term—and which deserve
rather careful examination.

Now in the make and nature of every man, however rude
or simple, whom we employ in manual labour, there are
some powers for better things: some tardy imagination,
torpid capacity for emotion, tottering steps of thought, there
are, even at the worst; and in most cases it is all our own
fault that they *are* tardy or torpid.

This is apparently simple enough and might be called
staple Ruskin, very obviously spaced, the groups being
almost exactly marked by the punctuation. They go 4, 3,
3, 4: then after the colon one hesitates whether to stress
"some," and one is brought up suddenly with the repeated
"there are"; finally after the semicolon the six words
almost without emphasis leave one with the sequent
threes, picking up the two threes ("torpid . . . emotion,"
"tottering . . . thought") in which the parallelism is
pointed up by alliteration. Then, going back, one decides
against stressing the ambiguous "some"—"some tardy
imagination" is a two-group, in asymmetrical balance
strengthened by the alliterating *t* with the following
three-groups and pairing off with the unemphatic twos
of "even . . . worst" and "most cases." The scheme is,
then: 4, 3, 3, 4; 2, 3, 3, (2); (2), 3, 3.

But Ruskin can do better than this—as for example,
among many others, in the conclusion of a sentence from
Stones of Venice, II, i:

   . . . to write her history
      on the white scrolls of the sea-surges
    and to word it in their thunder,

and to gather and give forth,
in the world-wide pulsation,
the glory of the West and of the East,
from the burning heart
of her Fortitude and Splendour.

Here the groups (2, 2+2, 2, 2, 2, 2, 3, 2, 2) are signaled by the phrasing; and it is worth noting how the lengthening of the three-group is almost inaudibly repeated in the lengthening of "burning heart" to "Fortitude and Splendour," like a double cadence. With all this careful balancing are the alliterating echoes: "write," "white," "-wide"; "word," "world" (with "-surges," "burning"); "gather," "give," "glory"; and the omripresent *r*'s—seventeen of them in the forty-eight words. This is of course coloratura prose, rather satiating in quantity but exceedingly skilful and impressive as a flourish.

Of a different sort is the opening sentence of De-Quincey's *Levana and Our Ladies of Sorrow:*

Oftentimes at Oxford I saw Levana in my dreams.

Here two movements balance on the medial "I saw." The first or prose reading has two stresses on each side. But the latent trochees (or perhaps one might even say dipodic foot) of "Oftentimes at" reveals an alternative movement of three beats, which is at once picked up and repeated in "Levana in my dreams"; which in turn absorbs "I saw" into a sequence of four iambs. Thus one's awareness of prose resists the metrical at first, though one is prepared for conscious artistry in the author; then the metrical obtrudes itself; and one ends in uncertainty about either reading or their combination.

Of still another kind is this sentence from Constance Holme's *The Lonely Plough:*

There were depths in her he could never fathom, finenesses
he might respect but never grasp, shades of feeling making
life vivid that he would always fail to seize.

The balance is not immediately apparent:

> depths in her   —never fathom
> finenesses   —respect but never grasp

shades of feeling making life vivid—always fail to seize

that is: 1 + 2, 1 + 3, 4 + 3, a gradation of 1, 1, 4 in
the first members and of 2, 3, 3, in the second, although the stylistic substitution of "fail to" for "never"
slightly shortens the last clause.

The next example (from Irving's *The Alhambra*)
illustrates contrast rather than balance, and with it a series
of curiously asymmetrical dependent phrases. It begins
as mere prose but soon signals its intention with the
parallel adjectives "luxuriant" and "voluptuous"—

Many are apt to picture Spain to their imaginations as a
sort of Southern region, decked out with the luxuriant charms
of voluptuous Italy. On the contrary, though there are exceptions in some of the maritime provinces, yet, for the most
part, it is a stern, melancholy country, with rugged mountains, and long sweeping plains destitute of trees, and indescribably silent and lonesome, partaking of the savage and
solitary character of Africa.

The second sentence begins also as mere prose and the
rhythmic movement sets in only with "it is a stern...."
Grammatically "country" is modified by the two adjectives and the compound prepositional phrase, and then by
two more adjectives and the participial adjective. (The
comma after "trees" seems to indicate this, rather than
that "silent" and "lonesome" go with "plains.") All of
which is complex enough though not difficult to follow

once the ambiguity of "silent and lonesome" is removed. But crossing these syntactical movements and sometimes conflicting with them is another grouping—

3   stern melancholy country
2   rugged mountains
3   and long sweeping plains
2   destitute of trees
3   and indescribably silent and lonesome
5   partaking of the savage and solitary character of Africa.

The alternation of 3, 2, 3, 2 does not correspond to the grammatical structure, for "destitute of trees" has a coda effect. The "stern melancholy country" and "long sweeping plains" are alike in sound but not in syntax; and for a final twist, the coda-like "destitute of trees" is expanded to a five-stress group (not $3 + 2$, but $1 + 3 + 1$) in which "savage and solitary character" seems to echo, but does not, the preceding three-groups of two adjectives plus noun. The result is something very complex, probably not calculated by Irving, yet highly interesting.

This coda-like shortening can be very effective: it was a favorite device of Pater's. A very simple form of it is

Then all the disciples left him, and fled.

It is slightly disguised in

And he went out and wept bitterly,

for the alliteration brings the two verbs together, leaving the adverb less closely attached to its verb.[4] The coda is longer in

And they heard the voice of the Lord God walking in the garden in the cool of the day.

Pater has a plain example in

Out of the secret places of a unique temperament he brought strange blossoms and fruits hitherto unknown; and for him, the novel impression conveyed, the exquisite effect woven, counted as an end in itself—a perfect end.

A less obvious use comes near the beginning of the famous Mona Lisa passage—

The presence that rose thus so strangely beside the waters, is expressive of what in the ways of a thousand years men had come to desire. Hers is the head upon which all "the ends of the world are come," and the eyelids are a little weary.

And again twice in his replica (so to say) of the Mona Lisa portrait, written a year later, contrasting Botticelli's madonnas with the Sistine Madonna and the Virgins of Fra Angelico—

At first, contrasting them with those, you may have thought that there was something in them mean or abject even, for the abstract lines of the face have little nobleness, and the colour is wan. For with Botticelli she too, though she holds in her hands the "Desire of all nations," is one of those who are neither for Jehovah nor His enemies; and her choice is on her face.

v

The periodic sentence is an obvious method of prolonging the rhythmic waves, but it is method easily abused. The virtue of a periodic sentence is that it keeps a number of related matters suspended in midair while we gradually master the relations, and then deposits the whole safely on the ground after the relations have been apprehended and the suspense gratified. Such a sentence is a pyramid held aloft as though poised on its apex, until, slowly turning, it finally comes to rest on its base. The method demands mastery or leads to trouble. Thus—

It is no exaggeration to say that Borrow was never, in the long years he spent in retirement at Oulton, happy.

Emphasis is purchased at too high a price. "Borrow was never happy" is one movement, "in the long years . . . at Oulton" is another. They can properly be harmonized, but thrusting the subordinate clause in so late is a kind of violence. On the other hand, the disturbing parenthesis in DeQuincey's

Death we can face; but, knowing as some of us do what is human life, which of us is it that without shuddering could (if consciously we were summoned) face the hour of birth?

is a deliberate postponement to increase the shock of the idea. A supreme example of the discordant parenthesis occurs, surprisingly enough, in one of Pater's most studiedly rhythmized sentences:

In him first appears the taste for what is *bizarre* or *recherché* in landscape; hollow places full of the green shadow of bituminous rocks, ridged reefs of trap-rock which cut the water into quaint sheets of light,—their exact antitype is in our own western seas; all the solemn effects of moving water.

With all the metrical effects, culminating in the final blank verse, the concealed balance of "the green shadow" and "bituminous rocks," and the exact balance of "ridged reefs of" and "quaint sheets of," Pater has first risked introducing the two foreign words and as if this were not enough he changes both tone and tune at the dash; nor is the echo "own western" sufficient compensation.

Again, take this sentence by Mr. Frank Swinnerton:

Whether it is that the characters have no intrinsic interest, or whether, in its attempt to give such a picture of the poor as Balzac gives of the French peasantry, or of such persons as La Cibot, in *Le Cousin Pons*, it loses original impulse, it is hard to say.

The original impulse of this sentence became lost in the series of "or-" members, quite lost in the last parenthesis. But the movement of such a sentence is always interesting and usually satisfying, provided the mind, as distinct from the ear, is not overtaxed. Here it is noteworthy that the rhythm seemed to require something before "is hard to say"; but there have been two "it's" already (beside the "its"), one expletive and one pronominal, and the simple "would be hard to say" not only expresses the meaning adequately but also satisfies the ear.

Both the good and the bad together are well illustrated by Ruskin:

People speak in this working age, when they speak from their hearts, as if houses and lands, and food and raiment were alone useful, and as if Sight, Thought, and Admiration were all profitless, so that men insolently call themselves Utilitarians, who would turn, if they had their way, themselves and their race into vegetables; men who think, as far as such can be said to think, that the meat is more than the life and the raiment than the body, who look to the earth as a stable and to its fruit as fodder; vinedressers and husbandmen, who love the corn they grind, and the grapes they crush, better than the gardens of the angels upon the slopes of Eden.

On this George Henry Lewes comments: "It is instructive to contrast the dislocated sentence [i.e., clause], 'who would turn, if they had their way, themselves and their race,' with the sentence which succeeds it, 'men who think, as far as such can be said to think, that the mean,' etc.

In the latter the parenthetic interruption is a source of power: it dams the current to increase its force; in the former the inversion is a loss of power; it is a dissonance and a diversion of the thought." But it is not a very good sentence for various reasons, among them perhaps the meanness of its sarcasm. It is of course not properly periodic, since with the clause "so that men insolently . . . ," where the sarcasm enters, it begins to trail away into another subject and so start over again for a new peak with the angels of Eden. There is a false parallelism between "who should turn, if . . ." and on the other hand "think, as far as . . . and look . . ." (without a parenthesis). But it is pulled together for its 'run on the avenue' when the several preceding "who's" are subsumed under "vinedressers and husbandmen" and followed by another "who-" clause with the asymmetrical balance of "corn they grind" and "grapes they crush" with "gardens of the angels" and "slopes of Eden." Until the semicolon the rhythm is false because the structure is confusing, and only part of the trouble is the contrast of the true and dissonant parentheses.

Now hear, finally, the organ tones of Hooker in a long slow periodic movement—a passage quoted by Saintsbury and praised for its "adaptation of the period *structure* of classical sentence to a large periodic rhythm; the abrupter and more intrusive parallelism or balance, as we find it in Lyly and others, being widened, softened, and moulded out into great undulating sweeps of phrase, rising, hovering, descending, with a wing-like motion."[5]

As therefore man doth consist of different and distinct parts, every part endued with manifold abilities which all have their several ends and actions thereunto referred; so there is in this great variety of duties which belong to men, that dependency and order by means whereof, the lower sustaining always the more excellent, and the higher perfecting the more base, they are in their times and seasons continued with most exquisite correspondence. Labours of bodily and daily toil purchase freedom for actions of religious joy, which benefit these actions requite with the gift of desired rest—a thing most natural and fit to accompany the solemn festival duties of honour which are done to God. For if those principal works of God, the memory whereof we use to celebrate at such times, be but certain tastes and [as]says, as it were, of that final benefit wherein our perfect felicity and bliss lieth folded up, seeing that the presence of the one doth direct our cogitations, thoughts, and desires towards the other, it giveth surely a kind of life, and addeth inwardly no small delight to those so comfortable anticipations, especially when the very outward countenance of that we presently do representeth, after a sort, that also whereunto we tend; as festival rest doth that celestial estate whereof the very heathens themselves, which had not the means whereby to apprehend much, did notwithstanding imagine that it must needs consist in rest, and have therefore taught that above the highest movable sphere there is no thing which feeleth alteration, motion, or change; but all things immutable, unsubject to passion, blest with eternal continuance in a life of the highest perfection, and of that complete abundant sufficiency within itself which no possibility of want, maim, or defect can touch.

vi

"And Marcian lived through the day he knew not how." This (from Gissing's *Veranilda*) is a sentence which few would praise for style: even in an historical novel of sixth-century Italy it has a stilted sound. It could have been: "And Marcian knew not how he lived through the day"—but so would have been much less emphatic. Or: "Marcian lived through the day knowing not how"—but so would have been much weaker. Or:

"How he lived through the day Marcian knew not"—
but still would have missed something. Or: "And Marcian lived through the day; how, he knew not"—which
would have been almost intolerably overemphatic. The
sound of each version is distinctly different, and each version, corresponding to a possible intended effect, has a
different influence on the reader's ear, even apart from
the grammatical arrangements.

It is these variations from the norm, from the simplest syntactic structure and the conventional order of
words, which offer to the prose writer his first opportunity to color his style and free his rhythm from the
obvious. Dionysius of Halicarnassus made the same observation long ago. The differences are those of rhythm:
"Certainly it is not in the thought or in the choice of
words."

When English developed from its first morpholog-
ical stage to a language with a minimum of inflectional
endings, it developed concurrently a more definite word
order than it had needed before. It may have lost something by the change, but it certainly gained something in
logic. Subject and its modifiers, predicate and its modifiers, object and its modifiers: nothing could be more logical. Any alteration of this fixed order produces a change
in the effect of the words. Sometimes the difference is
purely one of meaning, as "They once defended themselves successfully" (but can no longer do so) beside
"They defended themselves successfully once" (and once
only); or "She simply looked at him" (i.e., merely
looked) beside "She looked at him simply" (i.e., in a
simple, innocent fashion). Sometimes it is one of emphasis: "Only five of the conquerors fell" beside "Of the
conquerors only five fell"; and not merely is the second

statement more emphatic, more highly 'colored,' but there is in it also a slightly greater stress on "only." So with "Lord B. came in presently" and "Presently in came Lord B."; in the second form the stress has shifted from the verb to the prepositional adverb; because of its 'unnatural' position "in" carries more of the meaning than the verb. For in general the more important word, the word which answers the underlying question, comes last, and any alteration of this position brings in a new emphasis and supplants the expected rhythm. Adverbs of manner, being stronger than the verb they modify, follow their verb: "He came slowly towards her," "She looked wonderingly at him"; and to vary this order is to change, if ever so slightly, both sound and meaning. Moreover, there may be little difference in meaning between "I have brought back your umbrella" and "I have brought your umbrella back," but in the one "back" is spoken more clearly, and in the other (which most speakers would probably say is more natural) there is more of a tune—anapestic-dactylic, ∪∪′∪∪′∪∪. It may well be that the metrical smoothness is what makes the second seem more natural.

These are but a few illustrations of how we modify the normal forms of English expression, how we obtain the "continual slight novelty" in the interests of emphasis and rhythm. I will add one more, showing how an important word may be reduced in stress by its surroundings. "Far away on each hand stretch the rich pastures" *(The Mill on the Floss)* allows full emphasis on "stretch"; its full length and stress are felt. But in the complete sentence its force is largely lost: "Far away on each hand stretch the rich pastures, and the patches of dark earth, made ready for the seed of broad-leaved green crops, or touched already with the tint of the tender-bladed autumn-sown corn."[6]

vii

An author will always take special pains with his opening and closing paragraphs: the one prepares us for the effects which are to follow, the other re-emphasizes the tone of the whole preceding story or sums up the content or intent of the essay, chapter, or book.

The wórld in whìch we líve | has been váriously sáid and súng | by the most ingénious póets and philósophers: | thése redúcing it to fórmulae and chémical ingrédients, | thóse stríking the lýre, in hígh-sounding méasures for the hándiwork of Gód. What expérience supplíes is of míngled tíssue, | and the chóosing mínd has múch to rejéct, | before it can gét togéther the matérials for a théory. | Déw and thúnder, | destróying Átilla and the Spríng lámbkins, | belóngs to an órder of cóntrasts | which nó repetítion can assímilate. | There is an uncoúth, outlándish stráin | throughòut the wéb of the wórld, | as from a vexátious plánet in the hóuse of lífe. | Things are nót cóngruous and wear stránge disguíses: | the consúmmate flówer is fóstered out of dúng, | and after nóurishing itsélf a whíle | with héaven's délicate distillátions, | decáys agáin into indistínguishable sóil; | and with Cáesar's áshes, | Hámlet télls us, | the úrchins make dírt píes and fílthily besméar their cóuntenance. | Nay, the kíndly shíne of súmmer, | when trácked hóme with the scientífic spýglass, is fóund to íssue from the mòst porténtous níghtmare of the úniverse | — the gréat conflágrant sún: | a wórld of héll's squíbs, | tumúltuary, róaring alóud, inímical to lífe. | The sún itsélf is enóugh to disgúst a húman béing of the scéne which he inhábits; | and you would not fáncy there was a gréen or hábitable spót in a úniverse thus áwfully lighted úp. | And yèt it is by the bláze of súch a conflagrátion, | to which the fíre of Róme was but a spárk, | that we do áll our fíddling, and hold doméstic téa-parties at the árbour dóor.

This is a bit of conscious prose if ever there was one, the
opening paragraph of Stevenson's "Pan's Pipes"; it is a
deliberate attempt to write a reflective poem in prose,
but the deliberation is a little too forward. It is not to be
read rapidly, but to be savored slowly; therefore the half-
stresses are more emphatic than in less affected or more
natural writing, and I have not hesitated to mark them.
Perhaps it is unfair to ask a man to bear witness against
himself, yet here is the evidence: the groups indicated by
stresses are— 3 + 3 + 3: 3 + 2, 5 + 2. 4, 4 + 4.
2, 4, 3 + 3. 3 + 3, 4. 4: 4, 3 + 3, 5; 2, 2, 3 + 3.
1 + 3, 4, 6, 1, 2, 2. 6 + 2; 4 + 4. 4, 3, 2, 2 + 2. It
is too regular, though the skeleton is cunningly covered.
To point out the alliterations and the metrical patches
would be otiose: "the handiwork of God . . . the choosing
mind has much to reject . . . to which the fire of Rome
was but a spark" and so on, or the repetitions of "dew and
thunder . . . Caesar's ashes . . . Hamlet tells us"; but
the ascending gradation of "tumultuary, roaring aloud,
inimical to life" is worth remark.

One of the most successful final paragraphs in modern
fiction is that of Conrad's *The Heart of Darkness*. Mr.
Ford Madox Ford relates how he and Conrad argued
over it for three days, trying different arrangements of
punctuation and syntax, until one of the collaborators at
least was satisfied; for Mr. Ford adds: "It has always
seemed to me—and still seems—one of the most perfect
prose passages in the language." Here it is.

"We have lost the first of the ebb," said the Director
suddenly. I raised my head. The offing was barred by a
black bank of clouds and the tranquil waterway, leading to
the uttermost ends of the earth, flowed sombre under an
overcast sky—seemed to lead into the heart of an immense
darkness.

A passage so carefully composed should bear very close examination. Certainly one could defend a comma after "clouds"; and one can see why "the relatively harsh 'seemed' " was preferred to "the tender 'seeming' " (Mr. Ford's phrases), in order not to conflict with the participle "leading." But what can be said for the echoes of "lost . . . first," "ebb . . . head," "Black bank," "sombre under"? The rhythmic variations are very interesting, however. Anapests and five-stress groups predominate. The first of these groups contains sixteen syllables: " 'We have lost the first of the ebb,' said the Director suddenly"; the second, eleven syllables: "seemed to lead into the heart of an immense darkness." Interspersed with these are two groups of two beats and two of four beats, considerably varied: "I raised my head," "and the tranquil waterway"; and "leading to the uttermost ends of the earth," "flowed sombre under an overcast sky." The anapests are obvious: there are three in succession in "to the uttermost ends of the earth," and besides the others, two long or expanded anapests at the end: "into the heart of an immense." If all this were merely contrived by conscious labor (as one almost believes that Stevenson's was) it would be tiresome; but though it is plainly studied, the variety is achieved by ear and not by rule, and the rhythm is felt rather than seen. It stands therefore in admirable contrast to such sentences as Dr. Johnson's: "Of genius, that power which constitutes a poet; that quality without which judgement is cold and knowledge inert; that energy which collects, combines, amplifies, and animates; the superiority must, with some hesitation, be allowed to Dryden" ("Life of Pope"). In this passage of Conrad's the movement seems natural, the means of organization are never too apparent, the variations are genuinely subtle. The sequent anapests, with alliteration, of "-ing was barred by a black," are concealed by the harshly juxtaposed stresses of "black bank"; and the run of three anapests, already noted, is followed by the abrupt "flowed sombre." However freely one interprets Mr. Ford's story, the result stands; and perhaps the best praise one can give is that the paragraph never obtrudes its music but on repeated reading wins renewed approval.

viii

A sort of companion piece to Pater's Mona Lisa, though in a very different manner, is Carlyle's description of Giotto's portrait of Dante. I space it out to show some of the proportions.

After all commentaries, the Book itself is mainly what we know of him. The Book;—and one might add that Portrait commonly attributed to Giotto, which, looking at it, you cannot help inclining to think genuine, whoever did it.

To me it is a most touching face;	3
perhaps of all faces that I know, the most so.	4
Lonely there,	1
painted as on vacancy,	2
with the simple laurel wound round it;	3
the deathless sorrow and pain,	3
the known victory which is also deathless;—	4
significant of the whole history of Dante!	4
I think it is the mournfullest face that ever was painted from reality;	5
an altogether tragic, heart-affecting face.	4
There is in it, as foundation of it,	2
the softness, tenderness, gentle affection as of a child;	5
but all this is as if congealed into sharp contradiction,	4
into abnegation, isolation, proud hopeless pain.	5

A soft ethereal soul looking-out   4
so stern, implacable, grim-trenchant,   3
as from imprisonment of thick-ribbed ice!   3

Withal it is a silent pain too,   3
a silent scornful one: 2
the lip curled in a kind of godlike disdain   4
    of the thing that is eating-out his heart,—   3
as if it were withal a mean insignificant thing,   3
as if he whom it had power to torture and strangle   3
    were greater than it.   2

The face of one wholly in protest,   3
    and life-long unsurrendering battle,   3
        against the world.   1
Affectation all converted into indignation,   3
an implacable indignation;   2
slow, equable, silent, like that of a god!   4

The eye too, it looks-out as in a kind of surprise,   4
a kind of enquiry,   1
Why the world was of such a sort?   4

This is Dante: 2
so he looks,   2
this 'voice of ten silent centuries,'   4
and sings us 'his mystic unfathomable song.'   4

This is not a simple music, neither neatly balanced
nor smoothly flowing; nor is it without its own subdued
rhythms. It is not so plainly *studied* and wrought as
Pater's, yet it has certain subtleties which reveal themselves on close examination, and the apparent abruptnesses
are partially overcome by the equality of consecutive
divisions. There can be no question of the tonal effect as
finely suited to the suffering and indignation described.
As always there is some uncertainty about the half-
stresses: the slightest added emphasis, for example, on
that makes

slow, equable, silent, like that of a god

into a blank verse; and perhaps there is one in

tenderness, gentle affection as of a child.

Meter is evident in "the deathless sorrow and pain," in "congealed into sharp contradiction," and in "had power to torture and strangle were greater than it." There are concealed echoes in "godlike disdain of the thing . . . mean insignificant thing" and in "known victory . . . whole history," which are almost duplicated in "proud hopeless . . . lips curled in a." And one's ear catches the repeated 'foot' of four unstressed syllables between two stressed: "me it is a most touch- . . . victory which is al- . . . -nificant of the whole . . .-fection as of a child," which suggest meter but are part of the carefully preserved prose effect of several successive unemphasized syllables.

Elsewhere, Carlyle's *style*, his rough manners and harsh mannerisms, so much admired by some and detested by others, stands as the extreme pattern of stimulation and repose: violence and sweetness. Saintsbury praises the beauty of its rhythm but admits that it is "incomprehensible." It resembles—it anticipates, as one art often anticipates another—much modern music wherein the *effects* predominate and nearly everything else is sacrificed to power. Take the *Diamond Necklace:* "The story of the Diamond Necklace," said Froude, "is all told in that paper with the strictest fidelity, yet in a kind of musical way"; and a sentence from the opening paragraph might serve for epigraph: "A passion that explosively shivers asunder the Life it took rise in, ought to be regarded as considerable: more no passion, in the highest heydey of Romance, yet did." For mockery and grim laughter "that paper" is hardly to be surpassed: an extravaganza, a free fantasia *tumultuosissimamente*, with the grand finale of Cagliostro's "Occasional Discourse": "Thus spoke . . . the Arch-Quack Cagliostro"!

But, indeed, what of Du Barry? A foul worm; hatched by royal heat, on foul composts, into a flaming butterfly; now diswinged, and again a worm! Are there not Kings' Daughters and Kings' Consorts; is not Decoration the first wish of a female heart,—often also, if such heart is empty, the last? The Portuguese Ambassador is here, and his rigorous Pombal is no longer Minister: there is an Infanta in Portugal, purposing by Heaven's blessing to wed.—Singular! the Portuguese Ambassador, though without fear of Pombal, praises, but will not purchase.

This, garnish it and fringe it never so handsomely, is, alas, the intrinsic character of Prince Louis. A shameful spectacle: such, however, as the world has beheld many times; as it were to be wished, but is not yet to be hoped, the world might behold no more. Nay, are not all possible delirious incoherences, outward and inward, summed up, for poor Rohan, in this one incrediblest incoherence, that *he*, Prince Louis de Rohan, is named Priest, Cardinal of the Church? A debauched, merely libidinous mortal, lying there quite helpless, *dis*solute (as we well say); whom to see Church *Cardinal*, symbolical *Hinge* or main corner of the Invisible Holy in this World, an Inhabitant of Saturn might split with laughing,—if he did not rather swoon with pity and horror! . . .

Hark! Clang of opening doors! She issues, like the Moon in silver brightness, down the Eastern steeps. *La Reine vient!* What a figure! I (with the aid of glasses) discern *her*. O Fairest, Peerless! Let the hum of minor discoursing hush itself wholly; and only one successive rolling peal of *Vive la Reine*, like the movable radiance of a train of fire-works, irradiate her path. —Ye Immortals! She does, she beckons, turns her head this way!—"Does she not?" says Countess de Lamotte. —Versailles, the Œil-de

Bœuf, and all men and things are drowned in a Sea of Light; Monseigneur and that high beckoning Head are alone, with each other in the Universe.

Such is the music, a *scherzo agitato*, rhythmically (as in other ways) clattering and surging, its exclamatory jerkiness being ever softened and smoothed, if you listen for them, by little glides of tune, the shocks appeased by poetic hints and phrases, and, as it were, all possible incoherences of grammar and *style* resolved into an incomprehensible music—

> Like the moon in silver brightness,
> Down the eastern steeps.

ix

About Pater as a stylist much has been said and perhaps something is to be added, though it would not be in point here. His frequent long and disordered sentences, the product of a too sedulous revision for content without a corresponding regard for sound, are an annoyance to many and seriously detract from his reputation as a master of prose. But his *purpurei panni*, for which he carefully plumed his wings, are deservedly famous and masterpieces in their kind; though Mr. Welby very properly insisted that they were characteristic of only one of his styles. The gorgeousness of the Mona Lisa flight (to which I come presently) he tried to repeat in the Botticelli essay a year later:

At first, contrasting them with those, you may have thought that there was something in them mean or abject even, for the abstract lines of the face have little nobleness, and the colour is wan. For with Botticelli she too, though she holds in her hands the "Desire of all nations," is one of those who are neither for Jehovah nor for His enemies; and her choice

is on her face. The white light on it is cast up hard and
cheerless from below, as when snow lies upon the ground,
and the children look up with surprise at the strange white-
ness of the ceiling. Her trouble is in the very caress of the
mysterious child, whose gaze is always far from her, and
who has already that sweet look of devotion which men have
never been able altogether to love, and which still makes
the born saint an object almost of suspicion to his earthly
brethren. Once, indeed, he guides her hand to transcribe
in a book the words of her exaltation, the *Ave,* and the
Magnificat, and the *Gaude Maria,* and the young angels,
glad to rouse her for a moment from her dejection, are
eager to hold the inkhorn and to support the book. But the
pen almost drops from her hand, and the high cold words
have no meaning for her, and her true children are those
others, among whom, in her rude home, the intolerable
honour came to her, with that look of wistful inquiry on
their irregular faces which you see in startled animals—
gipsy children, such as those who, in Apennine villages, still
hold out their long, brown arms to beg of you, but on Sunday become *enfants du chœur,* with their thick black hair
nicely combed, and fair white linen on their sunburnt throats.

Most of the 'effects' here are simple: the coda-like "and
the colour is wan," repeated at the end of the next sentence, "and her choice is on her face"; the spondaic "she
too," "white light," and "cast up" (underlined somehow
by the staccato "hard and cheerless from below"), and
"snow lies," "still makes," "born saint," "rude home,"
immediately followed by the lilt of

> the children look up with surprise
> at the strange whiteness of the ceiling;

the metrical

> though she holds in her hands the "Desire";

the almost metrical

> he guides her hand to transcribe in a book
> the words of her exaltation;

and among many other dainties, the prolonged spondees (molossi, if you will) of the last sentence: "high cold words" and "still hold out" and "long, brown arms" and "thick black hair," culminating in the dipodic meter—

> and *fair white lin*en on the *sunburnt throats.*

Notable is the upward gradation of

> Once, indeed,
> he guides her hand
> to transcribe in a book
> the words of her exaltation:

two-stress units, the first with three syllables, the second with four, the third with six, the fourth with eight, followed immediately by

> the *Ave*,
> and the *Magnificat*,
> and the *Gaude Maria*,

one-stress units with three, six, and seven syllables.

Towards the end of the same essay there is, after a series of two- and three-stress groups, another instance of gradation which can hardly be accidental: one, two, three, four; two, three, four, five.

The same figure | —tradition connects it with Simonetta, | the Mistress of Giuliano de 'Medici | —appears again as Judith, | returning home | across the hill country, | when the great deed is over, | and the moment of revulsion come, | when the olive branch in her hand | is becoming a burden; as *Justice*,
sitting on a throne,
but with a fixed look of self-hatred
which makes the sword in her hand seem that of a suicide;

and again as Veritas,
in the allegorical picture of *Calumnia,*
where one may note in passing the suggestiveness of an
                                  accident
which identifies the image of Truth with the person of Venus.

In "The Poetry of Michelangelo" there is an interesting sentence in which the 'tricks' are somewhat different:

He loved the very quarries of Carrara, those strange grey
peaks which even at mid-day convey into any scene from
which they are visible something of the solemnity and still-
ness of evening, sometimes wandering among them month
after month, till at last their pale ashen colours seem to have
passed into his painting; and on the crown of the head of
the *David* there still remains a morsel of uncut stone, as if
by one touch to maintain its connection with the place from
which it was hewn.

Here we have a blank verse line to begin with and a
little later the tuneful

        on the crown of the head of the David . . .
        a morsel of uncut stone;

the rimes of "grey," "convey," "mid-day," the "-ing"
four times, the *p*-alliteration, the assonance of "stone"
and "hewn," and the balance of "strange grey peaks"
with "pale ashen colours."

But all Pater's resources of word music are in the Leonardo essay. For example, a gradation not quite so systematic as those in the Botticelli:

    Legions of grotesques sweep under his hand;
    for has not nature, too, her grotesques—
    the rent rock,
    the distorting lights of evening on lonely roads,
    the unveiled structure of man in the embryo,
    or the skeleton;

and the less striking picture of a young man

> seated in a stooping posture,
> his face in his hands,
> as in sorrow.

There are two couplets, one a little rough, the other quite conventional:

It was not in play that he painted that other Medusa,
the one great picture which he left behind him in Florence.

> Take again another head,
> still more full of sentiment.

(Compare Milton's

> Haste thee, nymph, and bring with thee
> Jest and youthful jollity:

Pater's lacks only the rime.) There is a long run of three-stress groups (with a few twos in alternation):

What may be called the fascination of corruption | penetrates in every touch | its exquisitely finished beauty. | About the dainty lines of the cheek | the bat flits unheeded. | The delicate snakes | seem literally strangling each other | in terrified struggle | to escape from the Medusa brain. | The hue which violent death | always brings with it . . .

There is an interesting pair of balanced 'feet'—

To him philosophy was to be something giving *strange swiftness* and *double sight,* divining the sources of springs beneath the earth. . . .

similar to the *"short cuts* and *odd byways"* in the preceding sentence.

For the sake of its special attractions at beginning and end, here is a longer passage from the same essay:

In him first appears the taste for what is *bizarre* or *recherché* in landscape: hollow places full of the green shadow of bituminous rocks, ridged reefs of trap-rock which cut the water into quaint sheets of light,—their exact antitype is in our own western seas; all the solemn effects of moving water. You may follow it springing from its distant source among the rocks on the heath of the *Madonna of the Balances,* passing, as a little fall, into the treacherous calm of the *Madonna of the Lake,* as a goodly river next, below the cliffs of the *Madonna of the Rocks,* washing the white walls of its distant villages, stealing out in a network of divided streams in *La Gioconda* to the seashore of the *Saint Anne*— that delicate place, where the wind passes like the hand of some fine etcher over the surface, and the untorn shells are lying thick upon the sand, and the tops of the rocks, to which the waves never rise, are green with grass, grown fine as hair. It is the landscape, not of dreams or of fancy, but of places far withdrawn, and hours selected from a thousand with a miracle of *finesse.* Through Leonardo's strange veil of sight things reach him so; in no ordinary night or day, but as in faint light of eclipse, or in some brief interval of falling rain at daybreak, or through deep water.

Here, first, the "green shadow of bituminous rocks" echoes the 'feet' noticed just above; the "quaint sheets of light" repeats the "ridged reefs of trap-." Then suddenly comes the bizarre parenthesis, with hardly adequate punctuation, interrupting both sound and sense; followed at once by the smooth metrical flow of "all the solemn effects of moving water." The fanciful idea of the next sentence proceeds with plain four- and five-stress groups, until "the seashore of *Saint Anne*" sets off a new flight: "that delicate place, where the wind passes . . . the untorn shells are lying thick . . . waves never rise . . . green with grass, grown fine as hair"—all skilfully chosen to please the sensitive ear as well as touch the visual imagination. Then comes the sentence which has fascinated every student of prose rhythm and which will be found in every

essay on the subject: a series of three-stress groups delicately modulated and shortened at the close with a veri-
table miracle of finesse. The last sentence brings a fresh
tune, the recurrent motif of which is ⏑ ⏑ ′ : "veil of
sight . . . reach him so . . . night or day . . . light of
eclipse . . . falling rain," varied at the end to "deep
water." Perhaps metrical symbols will show some of these
intricacies: I scan, beginning with "and the untorn
shells"—

```
  ⏑ ⏑ ′      ⏋ ′      ⏑ ⏋ ⏑ ′     ⏑ ⏑ ⏑ ′
  ⏑ ⏑ ′    ⏑ ⏑ ′     ⏑ ⏋ ⏑ ′      ⏋ ⏑ ′
    ⏑ ′      ⏑ ′        ⏋ ′         ⏑ ′

 ⏑ ⏑ ⏑ ′     ⏋ ′       ⏑ ′       ⏑ ⏑ ′ ⏑
          ⏑ ⏑ ′       ⏑ ′        ⏑ ′
            ⏑ ′        ⏑ ′      ⏑ ⏑ ⏑ ′ ⏑
                     ⏑ ⏑ ′     ⏑ ⏑ ⏑ ⏑ ′

          ⏑ ′            ′       ⏑ ′
            ′            ′       ⏑ ′
         ⏑ ⏑ ′     ⏑ ⏑ ⏑ ′      ⏑ ′
        ⏑ ⏑ ⏑ ′          ′     ⏑ ⏑ ′
         ⏑ ⏑ ′           ′       ′ ⏑ ⏑
           ⏑ ′      ⏑ ′       ⏑ ′ ⏑
                  ⏑ ⏑ ′         ′ ⏑
```

And all these, and many other curiosities of the essay,
are as practice work, as trial flights for the almost too
famous Monna Lisa paragraph, itself "a beauty wrought
out from within upon the [page], the deposit, little cell
by cell, of strange thoughts and fantastic reveries and exquisite passions." With the thoughts, fancies, and passions we are not concerned, save to remark that they are
an adequate support for the *bravura* of the prose; nor
with a general assay of the paragraph as literature, with
its wide historical background; but only with the mysteries of its rhythmic devices, so far as we can penetrate
them.

The presence that rose thus so strangely beside the

waters, is expressive of what in the ways of a thousand years men had come to desire. Hers is the head upon which all "the ends of the world are come," and the eyelids are a little weary. It is a beauty wrought out from within upon the flesh, the deposit, little cell by cell, of strange thoughts and fantastic reveries and exquisite passions. Set it for a moment beside one of those white Greek goddesses or beautiful women of antiquity, and how would they be troubled by this beauty, into which the soul with all its maladies has passed! All the thoughts and experience of the world have etched and moulded there, in that which they have of power to re-fine and make expressive the outward form, the animalism of Greece, the lust of Rome, the mysticism of the middle age with its spiritual ambition and imaginative loves, the return of the Pagan world, the sins of the Borgias. She is older than the rocks among which she sits; like the vampire, she has been dead many times, and learned the secrets of the grave; and has been a diver in deep seas, and keeps their fallen day about her; and trafficked for strange webs with Eastern merchants, and, as Leda, was the mother of Helen of Troy, and, as Saint Anne, the mother of Mary; and all this has been to her but as the sound of lyres and flutes, and lives only in the delicacy with which it has moulded the changing lineaments, and tinged the eyelids and the hands. The fancy of a perpetual life, sweeping together ten thou-sand experiences, is an old one; and modern philosophy has conceived the idea of humanity as wrought upon by, and summing up in itself, all modes of thought and life. Cer-tainly Lady Lisa might stand as the embodiment of the old fancy, the symbol of the modern idea.

The first sentence is built of two similar curves, each of six stresses, 'balanced' on the anapestic center "is ex-pressive of what." The first curve has three subdivisions, the second two; the general movement, in spite of the trochaic "waters," is iambic-anapestic or 'rising' rhythm. This is reversed in the next sentence: the rhythm is 'falling,' or trochaic-dactylic, again in spite of the iambic "are come," with a remarkable "dying fall" at the close. The rhythm is somewhat disturbed by the illogical emphasis forced upon "which" by the pause, so that there seem to be three unequal groups: the first with three stresses; the second, almost metrical, with four; and the third with three, although the slow tempo and the preceding meter combine to prolong the second syllable of "eyelids," making a four-stress group. To be noted also in the first sentence are the balance of "so strangely beside the wa-" and "the ways of a thousand years," and the shorter balance of "expressive of what" and "had come to desire." Similarly in the second sentence "Hers is the head upon which" matches "all the ends of the world" as well as "ends of the world are come." (This slight ambiguity goes with the double allusion, for though the quotation is from I Corinthians, there is a possible reminiscence of "all the ends of the world," Ps. 22: 27.) The third sentence is more regular, yet with a similar variation produced by the intrusive meter: the attention given to "out" and the iambic "within upon the flesh"; it might be read with a 'tie' over "wrought out" and a subordination of "upon," so that the grouping becomes 1, 3, 1, 3, 6, with a marked *rallentando*.

> It is a beauty
>   wrought out from within upon the flesh
> the deposit,
>   little cell by cell,
> of strange thoughts and fantastic reveries and
>   exquisite passions.

The following sentence begins rapidly (two stresses in eleven syllables); meets a sudden check with the triad "white Greek goddesses," which is expanded to "beautiful women of antiquity"; recovers some of the first tempo (three stresses in eleven syllables; though "and how would they be troubled by this beauty," if taken slowly is a tolerable blank verse); and is slowed down in the last group (four stresses in thirteen syllables) by the metrical sequence "the soul with all its maladies."

> All the thoughts and experience of the world
> have etched and moulded there

resembles half of a ballad stanza; the following run of unstressed syllables brings a lull; then with "the animalism of Greece" begins a formal series of 2-2-3 (or 2), 2, 2-3-2. To be noted here is also the balance of "the return of the Pagan" and "the sins of the Borgias."

The architectonic of the long sentence beginning "She is older," the climax of the paragraph, is very remarkable and is not entirely clear from Pater's punctuation. The first large division ends with the semicolon after "Mary" and consists of five parts; the second consists of two parts and continues to the full stop. The first part is a single simple group which may be read with three stresses or four according to the emphasis on "among which." The second "like the vampire" etc., has three groups with one, three, and three stresses respectively. The third has likewise seven stresses, but in two groups, the irregularity of the former being compensated by the metrical run of the latter: "keeps their fallen day about her." The fourth is shorter, five stresses, with "strange webs" to echo "deep seas" in the preceding part. The fifth has again seven stresses in two groups, each subdivided and balanced by the repetition of "the mother of" and mainly anapestic. The second division of the sentence (after "Mary;") seems more rapid because of the two long runs of seven unstressed syllables: "has been to her but as the" and "-icacy with which it has," which seem to bring down with an impetuous rush the accumulated ideas of the long first upward sweep and deposit them with a swift irony—"the sound of lyres and flutes." Finally, underlining the irony, comes the long-drawn cadence—already prepared for by "has moulded the changing lineaments"—"and tinged the eyelids and the hands," which courts an iambic tune. Change "eyelids" and the magic is gone: they are of course the eyelids which were "a little weary" at the beginning. Nor should the long linking balances be overlooked:

> A diver in deep seas and keeps their fallen . . .
> and trafficked for strange webs with Eastern merchants

and

> and keeps their fallen day about her . . .
> and tinged the eyelids and the hands

The remainder of the paragraph is anticlimax, certainly in what it says and similarly (I am sure) in rhythm. It is explanatory and almost apologetic; and the syllables hesitate. The groups are irregular and broken, and only remotely fit the meaning; the want of correspondence between sound and sense is easily apparent. The wings droop after the long flight.

Such are the movements as I hear them, of the successive sentences: the movement of the whole paragraph is less easy to report. Setting aside any question of the relation of Leonardo's picture and Pater's account of it, and thinking only of what Pater meant to tell us, can we find a principle of rhythmic structure in the paragraph organizing the various details? It begins with a double rising curve and descends in a shorter curve to the dying

fall of "the eyelids are a little weary." The same rise and
fall continue in the two following sentences, but on a
higher level, the first fairly regular, the second varied
with changes of tempo and sustained by a semicadence
at the exclamation point. The next sentence holds this
pitch with a stanzaic opening, sinks a moment, and rises
in a fivefold ascent from "the animalism of Greece" to
"the sins of the Borgias": that is, the curve is reversed.
Then for the climax come the long sweeps beginning
"She is older than the rocks," the peak at "all this," and
the slow subsidence of the sentence, a hundred and three
words long, to its ironic close. After which the paragraph
limps to a conclusion.

Pater's collective *Studies in the History of the Renaissance* was published in 1873, but the Leonardo essay had
appeared in the *Fortnightly* in 1869 and the Botticelli in
1870. Apropos of the volume, Swinburne wrote to
Morley:

I admire and enjoy Pater's work so heartily that I am somewhat shy of saying how much, ever since on my telling him
once at Oxford how highly Rossetti (D. G.) as well as myself estimated his first papers in the *Fortnightly*, he replied
to the effect that he considered them as owing their inspiration entirely to the example of my own work in the same
line. . . .[7]

The proof of this inspiration is not far to seek. Interest
in the Italian painters was general, and Pater was only
one of those who occupied themselves at the time with
Renaissance painting; but Swinburne's "Notes on Designs
of the Old Masters at Florence," which appeared in the
Fortnightly for July 1868, contains both matter and manner which must have 'inspired' Pater. With the matter,
especially the *femme fatale*, we are not now concerned:

a single illustration will do, one luckily containing a Pateresque note (italics mine):

The least thought of these men has in it something intricate and enormous, faultless as the formal work of their triumphant art must be. All mysteries of good and evil, all wonders of life and death, lie in their hands or at their feet. They have known the causes of things, *and are not too happy*.

In the preceding paragraph Swinburne had written of Leonardo's drawings:

Fair strange faces of women full of dim doubt and faint scorn; touched by the shadow of an obscure fate; eager and weary as it seems at once, pale and fervent with patience and passion; allure and perplex the eyes and thoughts of men. There is a study here of Youth and Age meeting; it may be, of a young man suddenly coming upon the ghostly figure of himself as he will one day be; the brilliant life in his face is struck into sudden pallor and silence, the clear eyes startled, the happy lips confused. A fair straight-featured face, with full curls fallen or blown against the eyelids; and confronting it, a keen, wan, mournful mask of flesh: the wise ironical face of one made subtle and feeble by great age.

Here you would think you were reading Pater at his most mannered—the series of five four-stress groups and a little later the three-stress groups. One misses the Swinburnian alliteration in Pater, nor would Pater have ventured the chiastic "allure and perplex the eyes and thoughts."

On one of Filippo Lippi's sketches Swinburne has:

Her face is very young, more faultless and fresher than the first forms and colours of morning; her pure mouth small and curved, cold and tender; her eyes, set with an exquisite mastery of drawing in the clear and gracious face, seem to show actual colour of brilliant brown in their shapely and lucid pupils, under their chaste and perfect eyelids; her hair is deeply drawn backwards from the sweet low brows and small rounded cheeks, heaped and hidden away under a knotted veil whose flaps fall on either side of her bright round throat.

Again, on Andrea del Sarto:

His art is to me as the Tuscan April in its temperate days, fresh and tender and clear, but lulled and kindled by such air and light as fills the life of the growing year with fire. At Florence only can one trace and tell how great a painter and how various he was. There only but surely there can the influence and pressure of the things of time on his immortal spirit be understood; how much of him was killed or changed, how much of him could not be.

This might almost be Pater on Leonardo. At any rate, the strictly balanced groups are here as in Pater, rhythmized almost to the metrical, and if anything more obvious to eye and ear. For Pater's style, that is, the style for which he is famous, is quieter than Swinburne's—a stained-glass style, sometimes a bit awkward in design (the leading too prominent), but with its own beauty, and letting in but a limited amount of light.

"There are such mysterious things," said Pater. "Take that saying: 'Come unto me, all ye that are weary and heavy-laden.' How can you explain that? There is a mystery in it—a something supernatural." Part of the mystery may be due to the sacred associations, but there remains a magic which can be only partly explained.

Come unto me all ye that labour and are heavy laden, and I will give you rest. Take my yoke upon you, and learn of me; for I am meek and lowly in heart: and ye shall find rest unto your souls. For my yoke is easy and my burden is light.

Read it first for the latent meter. Note the repetition

of the theme: "Come unto me | all ye that la- | . . . lowly in heart | . . . burden is light"; and expanded in "rest unto your souls." Note the quasi-blank verse, "all ye that labour and are heavy laden," followed by three iambs, "and I will give you rest"; and then the other iambs, "and learn of me . . . for I am meek and low- . . . and ye shall find . . . my yoke is eas-." Running counter to these is the trochaic or falling rhythm initiated by "Come unto . . . heavy laden . . . Take my yoke upon you . . . meek and lowly . . . yoke is easy."

Then there are similarly two woven melodies based upon the distinction, here very marked, of stronger and weaker stresses:

Come unto me all ye that labour and are heavy laden, and I will give you rest. Take my yoke upon you, and learn of me; for I am meek and lowly in heart: and ye shall find rest unto your souls. For my yoke is easy and my burden is light.

When read as prose purely, as of course it should be read, the passage falls into unequal groups of 1 (or 1½), 4, 3, 3 + 2, 4, 3, 2 + 2 stresses. Note the equivalence of the fours:

> all ye that labour and are heavy laden
> for I am meek and lowly in heart
> For my yoke is easy and my burden is light

and the threes:

> and I will give you rest
> and ye shall find rest unto your souls.

But owing to the mingling of stronger and weaker stresses, this method of reading yields less than usual.

It is to this mingling and the latent metrical tunes that the "supernatural" effect is due—so far as the mystery can be unveiled.

Sir John Squire, in his *Reflections and Memories*, quotes the following passage, and adds in its praise: "that very last word 'aliment' is perfect in weight and movement: try to substitute any of its so-called synonyms for it and Pater's sensitive taste and cunning will be evident."

That a Numa, and his age of gold, would return, has been the hope or dream of some, in every period. Yet if he did come back, or any equivalent of his presence, he could but weaken, and by no means strike through, that root of evil, certainly of sorrow, of outraged human sense, in things, which one must carefully distinguish from all preventible accidents. Death, and the little perpetual daily dyings, which have something of its sting, he must necessarily leave untouched. And, methinks, that were all the rest of man's life framed entirely to his liking, he would straightway begin to sadden himself, over the fate—say, of flowers! For there is, there has come to be since Numa lived perhaps, a capacity for sorrow in his heart, which grows with all the growth, alike of the individual and of the race, in intellectual delicacy and power, and which *will* find its aliment.

Such a paragraph, says Sir John, "is all his own, and reminds us of nobody except his successors. The mere noise of him read, with only a half-attention to his meaning, is like the sound of fountains in secluded gardens, or of trees faintly rustling on a summer afternoon, or of a fire burning quietly in a curtained night, or of bees or of sleepy birds, or of a melancholy wind." This is high praise, of course, and being itself somewhat Pateresque in manner shows the writer's allegiance. But it is a manner to be used only in its own place—a place of quiet fountains and rustling trees and sleepy birds and a melancholy wind. Its charm and its justification is that it matches its matter; its hesitancies and affectations belong with the uncertainties of its subject. You might call it a shadowy prose for shadowy meanings; and then its rhythm is perfect, even to the dying fall of the last word. But it is a limited prose, as all prose is limited; and one must be careful not to suggest condemnation by the stricture; as Ruskin's characteristic prose is limited to Ruskin's characteristic ideas or matter; or as Johnson's or as De-Quincey's or as Matthew Arnold's or as the prose of yesterday's newspaper.[8]

The 'successors' of Pater in this very special manner are not numerous, but they are sometimes unexpected. Here is a specimen from Meredith *(Vittoria)*, a description of Mazzini's eyes, and it was published two years before Pater's essay on Leonardo:

The eyes were dark as the forest's border is dark; not as night is dark. Under favourable lights their colour was seen to be a deep rich brown, like the chestnut, or more like the hazel-edged sunset brown which lies upon our western rivers in the winter floods, when night begins to shadow them.

And here is another, from James Joyce *(A Portrait of the Artist as a Young Man)*:

The veiled windless hour had passed and behind the panes of the naked window the morning light was gathering. A bell beat faintly very far away. The bird twittered; two birds, three. The bell and the bird ceased: and the dull white light spread itself east and west, covering the world, covering the roselight in his heart.

Only "roselight" is new; Pater would have hesitated over that. But he would have rejoiced in the rime, the molossus, and the epithet "naked"; and he would have been proud (in his way) of the arcane balance in "The bird twittered; two birds, three."

x

Edmund Burke was not exactly a stylist, but an orator, an orator in the eighteenth-century tradition of fine rhetoric. His *Letter to a Noble Lord*[9] has been described as "perhaps the most brilliant exhibition of sarcastic powers in the whole range of English prose," and the famous Windsor passage has excited no little comment. It will be recalled that when in 1795 the Duke of Bedford attacked the grant of his pension, Burke was sixty-six years old, a retired public servant, infirm and despondent. He had just finished the six-year-long trial of Warren Hastings, his only son had but recently died, and he himself had but two years to live. The attack moved him to a last great effort, to which he devoted great labor and which he is said to have regarded as his most successful piece of writing. The *Letter* is not all in the same elaborate style. Some of it is as pointedly balanced as anything in Dr. Johnson.

All this, in effect, I think, but am not sure, I have said elsewhere. It cannot at this time be too often repeated; line upon line; precept upon precept; until it comes into the currency of a proverb, *to innovate is not to reform*. The French revolutionists complained of everything; they refused to reform anything; and they left nothing, no, nothing *unchanged*. The consequences are *before* us,—not in remote history; not in future prognostication: they are about us; they are upon us. They shake the public security; they menace private enjoyment. They dwarf the growth of the young; they break the quiet of the old. If we travel, they stop our way. They infest us in town; they pursue us to the country. Our business is interrupted; our repose is troubled; our pleasures are saddened; our very studies are poisoned

and perverted, and knowledge is rendered worse than igno-
rance, by the enormous evils of this dreadful innovation.

When he contrasts the source of his pension with the
origin of Bedford's wealth, Burke begins: "Mine was
from a mild and benevolent sovereign; his from Henry
the Eighth" and then continues through several paragraphs of unequal length with "mine" and "his" like the
swing of a pendulum, ending with "Thus stands the account of the comparative merits of the Crown grants
which compose the Duke of Bedford's fortune as balanced
against mine." Just after the great Windsor flight there
is another, more conventional use of refrain.

If he pleads the merit of having performed the duty of
insurrection against the order he lives, (God forbid he ever
should,) the merit of others will be to perform the duty of
insurrection against him. If he pleads (again God forbid he
should, and I do not suspect he will) his ingratitude to the
Crown for its creation of his family, others will plead their
right and duty to pay him in kind. They will laugh, indeed they will laugh at his parchment and his wax. His
deeds will be drawn out with the rest of the lumber of his
evidence room, and burnt to the tune of *ça ira* in the courts
of Bedford (then Equality) house.

When he recalls his son's death he is capable of moving pathos.

Had it pleased God to continue to me the hopes of succession, I should have been, according to my mediocrity,
and the mediocrity of the age I live in, a sort of founder
of a family: I should have left a son, who, in all points in
which personal merit can be viewed, in science, in erudition,
in genius, in taste, in honour, in generosity, in humanity, in
every liberal sentiment, and every liberal accomplishment,
would not have shown himself inferior to the Duke of Bedford, or to any of those whom he traces in his line. . . . At

this exigent moment, the loss of a finished man is not easily supplied.

But a disposer whose power we are little able to resist, and whose wisdom it behoves us not at all to dispute, has ordained it in another manner, and (whatever my querulous weakness might suggest) a far better. The storm has gone over me; and I lie like one of those old oaks which the late hurricane has scattered about me. I am stripped of all my honours, I am torn up by the roots, and lie prostrate on the earth! There, and prostrate there, I most resignedly recognize the Divine justice, and in some degree submit to it. But whilst I humble myself before God, I do not know that it is forbidden to repel the attacks of unjust and inconsiderate men. . . . I am alone. I have none to meet my enemies at the gate. Indeed, my lord, I greatly deceive myself, if in this hard season I would give a peck of refuse wheat for all that is called fame and honour in the world. . . . I live in an inverted order. They who ought to have succeeded me are gone before me. They who should have been to me as posterity are in the place of ancestors. . . .

And there are other fine things, not in the *ore rotundo* manner; among them a paragraph beginning "Their geographers and geometricians . . . ," the close of which Carlyle might have been proud to have written. But supreme in its very special kind is the picture of Windsor Castle as the protection of England.

Such are *their* ideas; such *their* religion, and such *their* law. But as to *our* country and *our* race, as long as the well compacted structure of our church and state, the sanctuary, the holy of holies of that ancient law, defended by reverence, defended by power, a fortress at once and a temple, shall stand inviolate on the brow of the British Sion—as long as the British monarchy, not more limited than fenced by the orders of the state, shall, like the proud Keep of Windsor, rising in the majesty of proportion, and girt with the double belt of its kindred and coeval towers, as long as this awful

structure shall oversee and guard the subjected land—so
long the mounds and dykes of the low, fat, Bedford level
will have nothing to fear from all the pickaxes of all the
levellers of France. As long as our sovereign lord the king,
and his faithful subjects, the lords and commons of this
realm,—the triple cord, which no man can break; the solemn, sworn, constitutional frank-pledge of this nation; the
firm guarantees of each others being, and each others rights;
the joint and several securities, each in its place and order, for
every kind and every quality, of property and of dignity—
As long as these endure, so long the duke of Bedford is
safe: and we are all safe together—the high from the
blights of envy and the spoliations of rapacity; the low from
the iron hand of oppression and the insolent spurn of contempt. Amen! and so be it; and so it will be,

> Dum domus Æneæ Capitoli immobile saxum
> Accolet; imperiumque pater Romanus habebit.

"This," says DeQuincey, "was the sounding passage
which Burke alleged as the *chef d'œuvre* of his rhetoric";
and DeQuincey did not altogether approve. Hazlitt is
fuller in his comment but rather general in his praise.

Nothing can well be more impracticable to a simile than
the vague and complicated idea which is here embodied in
one; yet how finely, how nobly it stands out, in natural
grandeur, in royal state, with double barriers round it to
answer for its identity, with "buttress, frieze, and coign of
'vantage" for the imagination to "make its pendant bed and
procreant cradle," till the idea is confounded with the object
representing it—the wonder of a kingdom; and then how
striking, how determined the descent, "at one fell swoop,"
to the "low, fat, Bedford level!" Poetry would have been
bound to maintain a certain decorum, a regular balance between these two ideas; sterling prose throws aside all such
idle respect to appearances, and with its pen, like a sword,
"sharp and sweet," lays open the naked truth. . . . Burke's

execution, like that of all good prose, savours of the texture of what he describes, and his pen glides or drags over the ground of his subject, like the painter's pencil. . . . I never pass Windsor but I think of this passage in Burke. . . .

But you notice, though Hazlitt plays with Burke's image and adorns it with snatches from Shakespeare, his one *critical* note of praise is for the amalgamation of all Burke's details with the general idea. The rest is metaphor.

Saintsbury is almost fulsome (pp. 279 f.).

It would take pages to bring out even the most strictly rhythmical characteristics of this wonderful *tour de force;* for there is hardly a word, save the merest particles, which does not contribute to the effect. The antithetic emphasis of "their" and "our"; the arrangement of "ideas," "religion," and "law"; the climax of the clause from "But as" to "Sion," and the parallel description of Windsor itself; the splendour of the "kindred and coeval towers"; the touch of the *xenon*—the strange arresting word—in "frank-pledge"; the ironic drawl of "the low | fat | Bedford | level"; the ordered processional and recessional of cadences to the close —all this cannot be beaten in the style. You may like some other style better if you please: I myself prefer several others. But if you do not like this, if you do not see the mastery and the beauty of this, there is a blind facet to your eye for style, a deaf spot in the drum of your ear for rhythm.

For the other side, hear Vernon Lee. Vernon Lee called the passage "a model of the inefficacious," saving the finale, "Amen! . . ." She complained that the fortress, temple, towers, and so on, which should be "sitting still," are "rambling vaguely all over the place," while the reader is following them through a series of parentheses and among the "qualifying sentences." (One sentence, please.) "The Windsor simile is thought *of*, not thought

in. . . . Least of all, had he really seen the towers of
Windsor arise as the symbol of British monarchy, would
he have been able to think of Bedfordshire from the
merely topographical and agricultural point of view, as
'low' and 'fat'?" (pp. 151 f.).

One thing at least is notable in these obiter dicta:
they recognize a general splendor of the rhetoric, a mag-
niloquence, but they are either vague or themselves rhetorical as to the rest. Hazlitt makes a point, Saintsbury
emphasizes the rhythms—he has scanned the whole passage; and those who find his method helpful should avail
themselves of that advantage. Only Vernon Lee attempts
to grapple with details, and the result is, if one accept
her strictures, damaging. Perhaps she missed Burke's
sarcasm; certainly she dislikes rhetoric; but she is more
concerned with the images and the argument than with
the sound. The question remains: is the music so loud as
to drown the meaning? is there a proper harmony between the rhythms and the ideas they accompany?

The first principle of Burke's intended effect is the
contrast of the short emphatic opening (threefold repetition of three-beat groups, with decreasing number of
syllables) and of the similar conclusion (threefold repetition of one-beat groups, with increasing number of syllables), with the long undulant sweeps of the sentence in
between. The solemn fanfare of the Latin hexameters is
of course outside the rhythm of the English passage. The
strong stresses of the first sentence are carried forward
by the emphatic "our." Then comes the formal device on
which all the rest is built: "as long as . . . so long." This
consists of two long waves, the first slightly longer than
the second, each with a complex rise, and a shorter summary before the first descent. Then the formula is re-

peated, this time with only two "as long as" clauses, one long, the other very short, leading to the final "so long." The simplicity of the main structure is offset by the variations of balance and antithesis, parallel and parenthesis, within the larger parts. But it is not the complexity of the inner rhythms which makes the long sentence remarkable; it is the length of the long curves, their building up, descent, rebuilding, and final descent.

The general shape and the lesser involutions may be shown clearly by spacing out the whole, with numbers at the right indicating by stresses the relative length of the parts. These numbers further reduced, reveal the comparative sizes of the curves: 22, 19, 6 for the first "as long as" members, and 13 for the first "so long"; then 36, 2 for the second "as long as" members, and 18 for the final "so long."

Such are *their* ideas	3
such *their* religion and	3
such *their* law.	3
But as to *our* country and *our* race	4
as long as the well compacted structure of our church	
and state	5
the sanctuary	1
the holy of holies of that ancient law	4
defended by reverence	2
defended by power	2
a fortress at once and a temple	3
shall stand inviolate on the brow of the British Sion	5
as long as the British monarchy	2
not more limited than fenced by the orders of	
the state	5
shall	
like the proud keep of Windsor	3
rising in the majesty of proportion and	3

girt with the double belt of its kindred and
coeval towers 6

as long as this awful structure 2
shall oversee and guard the subjected land 4
so long the mounds and flats of the low fat Bedford level 6
will have nothing to fear from all the pickaxes of
all the levellers of France 7

as long as our sovereign Lord the King and his faithful
subjects 5
the lords and commons of this realm 3
the triple cord which no man can break 4
the solemn sworn constitutional frank-
pledge of this 5
the firm guarantees of each other's being
and each other's rights 6
the joint and several securities 3
each in its own place and order 4
for every kind and every quality of property and of dignity 6

as long as these endure 2

so long the Duke of Bedford is safe 3
and we are all safe together 3
the high from the blights of envy and the spoliations of rapacity 5
the low from the iron hand of oppression and the
insolent spurn of contempt. 7

Amen
and so be it
and so it will be
Dum domus Æneæ. . . .

But the question cannot be avoided, whether the ideas
are commensurate with the soaring sound. Hazlitt saw a
noble grandeur in the comparison of Windsor Castle and
the British Monarchy; DeQuincey admitted an element
of fancy, no doubt in the Coleridgean sense. It is a

fanciful idea which taken seriously, as Burke took it, is
susceptible of dignified if not grandiose treatment; and
it is particularly useful to Burke by its contrast with the
Bedford level. But Burke, not content with this, lavishes
synonyms for church and state, all standing on the brow
of the British Sion. This out-Miltons Milton's

> deep on his front engraven
> Deliberation sat and public care,

of Beelzebub, without Milton's justification. (Vernon
Lee objected to "stand.") Later, strong language piles up
at some risk of inconsistency: king, subjects, and Parlia-
ment as a triple cord, which is a frank-pledge *(xenon* indeed), then guarantees and securities. The blights of
envy, the hand of oppression, and the spurn of contempt
are staple 'eighteenth-century'; the "double belt of its
kindred and coeval towers" is satisfying, if not breath-
taking, for any century; and the rhythmical delicacy of
"the low, fat, Bedford level" (it pleased Saintsbury)
must have been even more effective then than now. The
question of adequacy is thus answered: the rhythm is,
like the style, more pretentious than subtle, more oratorical than eloquent. The rhythmic structure is, if anything, better than the ideas and language; but when to
these is joined the organ tone of sarcasm, the elaboration
seems entirely justified and the rhythm is found to be
a necessary support for what might sink without it.

xi

One hesitates to include Landor in such a study as
this, lest one incur, and justly, the stricture which Mr.
Cyril Connolly, no doubt justly, made upon Dr. Richards. In his *Principles of Literary Criticism* Richards
quotes Landor's

On perceiving the countryman, she drew up her feet gently, and squared her mouth, and rounded her eyes, slumberous with content, and they looked, he said, like sea-grottoes, obscurely green, interminably deep, at once awakening fear and stilling and suppressing it.

And this, said Mr. Connolly, appeared to him like an oasis in the *Principles*. It is certainly a beautiful sentence, one to be felt rather than analyzed; but the musical movement is evident in its grouping of stresses ($2 + 2$), in its hidden rime, and in its long-drawn-out cadence, faintly forecast by the one word "gently."

On perceiving the countryman, she drew up her feet
    gently,
and squared her mouth, and rounded her eyes,
    slumberous with content,
    and they looked, he said,
    like sea-grottoes,
    obscurely green, interminably deep,
      at once awakening fear and stilling and
      suppressing it.[10]

Yet one must not omit the one writer who is most praised and admired of all for his prose rhythms. Mr. Morley Roberts, in his memories of Gissing, tells us, for example, that the *Imaginary Conversations* "possess to the full the two great qualities which most delighted him [Gissing]. It is redolent of the past, and those classic conversations were his chief joy; but above and beyond this, there was the most eminent quality of Landor's rhythms. I have often heard him read aloud from 'Aesop and Rhodope', and have even more often heard him quote without the book the passage which runs 'There are no fields of amaranth on this side of the grave; there are no voices, O Rhodope, that are not soon mute however

tuneful; there is no name, with whatever emphasis of
passionate love repeated, of which the echo is not faint
at last.'" Here indeed, "it may be, we have Landor's
rhythm at its loveliest." It is from the first of the two
Conversations of Æsop and Rhodopè and should be read
in its context. "But, Æsop," says Rhodopè, "you should
never say the thing that is untrue."

Æsop. We say and do and look no other all our lives.

Rhodopè. Do we never know better?

Æsop. Yes; when we cease to please, and to wish it;
when death is settling the features, and the cerements are
ready to render them unchangeable.

Rhodopè. Alas! alas!

Æsop. Breathe, Rhodopè, breathe again those painless
sighs: they belong to thy vernal season. May thy summer
of life be calm, thy autumn calmer, and thy winter never
come.

Rhodopè. I must die then earlier.

Æsop. Laodameia died; Helen died; Leda, the beloved
of Jupiter, went before. It is better to repose in the earth
betimes than to sit up late; better, than to cling pertinaciously to what we feel crumbling under us, and to protract
an inevitable fall. We may enjoy the present while we are
insensible of infirmity and decay: but the present, like a
note in music, is nothing but as it appertains to what is past
and what is to come. There are no fields of amaranth on
this side of the grave: there are no voices, O Rhodopè, that
are not soon mute, however tuneful: there is no name, with
whatever emphasis of passionate love repeated, of which
the echo is not faint at last.

Not all, of course, is like this; but this, though distinctly a gold and purple miniature, is not so different
or special as to seem out of place, to seem artificial and
appliquéd. As the thought becomes more poetical, the
language becomes more musical. Just as music is not

merely a succession of tunes, so the *Conversations* have their passage work along with their melodies, and Landor rarely fails to get the right effect at the right moment. Witness the finale of the second of the two Æsop conversations.

If, turning back, I could overpass the vale of years, and could stand on the mountain-top, and could look again far before me at the bright ascending morn, we would enjoy the prospect together; we would walk along the summit hand in hand, O Rhodopè, and we would only sigh at last when we found ourselves below with others.

But most of all, one should take Landor at his even best, his best level, without special coloring and without careless ease; for example, such a passage as the close of a paragraph from *Aspasia* (CLXXVI, "Aspasia to Anaxagoras"):

The business of philosophy is to examine and estimate all those things which come within the cognizance of the understanding. Speculations on any that lie beyond are only pleasant dreams, leaving the mind to the lassitude of disappointment. They are easier than geometry and dialectics; they are easier than the efforts of a well-regulated imagination in the structure of a poem. These are usually held forth by them as feathers and thistle-down; yet condescend they nevertheless to employ them; numerals as matter and mind; harmony as flute and fiddle-strings to the dances of the stars. In their compositions they adopt the phraseology and curtesy to the cadences of poetry. Look nearer; and what do you see before you? the limbs of Orpheus, bloodless, broken, swollen, and palpitating on the cold and misty waters of the Hebrus. Such are the rhapsodical scraps in their visionary lucubrations. They would poison Homer, the purest and soundest of moralists, the most ancient and venerable of philosophers, not out of any ill-will to him, but out of love to the human race. There is often an enchantment in their sentences, by which the ear is captivated, and against which the intellectual powers are disciplined to struggle; and there is sometimes, but very rarely, a simplicity of manner, which wins like truth. But when ambition leads them towards the poetical, they fall flat upon thorny ground. No writer of florid prose was ever more than a secondary poet. Poetry, in her high estate, is delighted with exuberant abundance, but imposes on her worshipper a severity of selection. She has not only her days of festival, but also her days of abstinence, and, unless upon some that are set apart, prefers the graces of sedateness to the revelry of enthusiasm. She rejects, as inharmonious and barbarous, the mimicry of her voice and manner, by obstreperous and argute grammarians, and she scatters to the winds the loose fragments of the schools.

VII

Rhythm and A-Rhythm

i

A METHOD MIGHT BE expected to work in both directions, to detect the presence of rhythmic qualities and to demonstrate their absence. But it is not so. For rhythm is a positive, and it is impossible to exhibit what does not exist. Newman is a good "case." His style is regularly praised, though seldom, I believe, for its rhythm. It has many excellences. Elton calls it "a great philosophical style—*manqué*." It has poetic and purplish passages; it has energy and weight and usually clearness —and above all sincerity. Newman is, as Elton says, again, "the least mannered writer of his time." But his words rarely flow; his written language is like his oral delivery, staccato. Not always, to be sure; but take this from "What is a University?":

I allow all this, and much more; such certainly is our popular education, and its effects are remarkable. Nevertheless, after all, even in this age, whenever men are really serious about getting what, in the language of trade, is called "a good article," when they aim at something precise, something refined, something really luminous, something really large, something choice, they go to another market; they avail themselves, in some shape or other, of the rival method, the ancient method, of oral instruction, of present communication between man and man, of teaching instead of learning, of the personal influence of a master, and the humble initiation of a disciple, and, in consequence, of great centres of pilgrimage and throng, which such a method of education necessarily involves. This, I think, will be found to hold good in all those departments or aspects of society, which possess an interest sufficient to bind men together, or to constitute what is called "a world." It holds in the political world, and in the high world, and in the religious world; and it holds also in the literary and scientific world.

There is only one stretch of more than ten consecutive words without a pause or mark of punctuation. There is almost a sense of improvising and patching, of halting movement, backing and filling. Moreover, the examples which Elton gives of his "plangent tones" and "musical voice" are of the same jerky sort; their plangency is in the ideas not in the sound.

The year is worn out; spring, summer, autumn, each in its turn, have brought their gifts and done their utmost; but they are over, and the end is come. All is past and gone, all has failed, all has sated. We are tired of the past; we would not have the seasons longer; and the austere weather which succeeds, though ungrateful to the body, is in tone with our feelings and acceptable.

Life passes, riches fly away, popularity is fickle, senses decay, the world changes, friends die. One alone is constant: One alone is true to us; One alone can be true; One alone can be all things to us; One alone can supply our needs.

It is much the same with another example, except that the members are a little longer—

She [the Church] holds that, unless she can, in her own way, do good to souls, it is no use her doing anything; she holds that it were better for sun and moon to drop from heaven, for the earth to fail, and for all the many millions who are upon it to die of starvation in extremest agony, so far as temporal affliction goes, than that one soul, I will not say should be lost, but should commit one single venial sin, should tell one wilful untruth, though it harmed no one, or steal one poor farthing without excuse. She considers the action of this world and the action of the soul simply incommensurate, viewed in their respective spheres; she would rather save the soul of one single wild bandit of Calabria, or whining beggar of Palermo, than draw a hundred miles of railroad through the length and breadth of Italy, or carry out a sanitary reform, in its fullest details, in every city of Sicily, except so far as these great national works tended to some spiritual good beyond them.

"In the form," says our critic, "everything here is well; the diction, the movement, the simple artful rise and fall, the valuing of the vowels." Is it so?

Take the famous paragraph from the *Apologia* begining "To consider the world in its length and breadth"— what is it but a series of short units, climactic in its arrangement of pictures, but with little attention to the curves of sound, culminating in "all this is a vision to dizzy and appal" and closing with the plain coda, "and inflicts upon the mind the sense of a profound mystery, which is absolutely beyond human solution"? Or take the equally well-known paragraph on the classics, from the *Grammar of Assent*. I space it out, to reveal the length and shortness of the members.

Let us consider,
too,
how differently young and old are affected by the words of
    some classic author,
such as Homer or Horace.
Passages,
which to a boy are but rhetorical common-places,
neither better nor worse than a hundred others,
which any clever writer might supply,
which he gets by heart and thinks very fine,

and imitates,
as he thinks,
successfully,
in his own flowing versification,
at length come home to him,
when long years have passed,
and he has had experience of life,
and pierce him,
as if he had never before known them,
with their sad earnestness and vivid exactness.
Then he comes to understand how it is
that lines,
the birth of some chance morning or evening at an Ionian
        festival,
or among the Sabine hills,
have lasted generation after generation,
for thousands of years,
with a power over the mind,
and a charm which the current literature of his own day,
with all its obvious advantages,
is utterly unable to rival.
Perhaps this is the reason of the mediæval opinion about
        Virgil,
as of a prophet or a magician;
his single words and phrases,
his pathetic half-lines,
giving utterance,
as the voice of Nature herself,
to that pain and weariness,
yet hope of better things,
which is the experience of her children in every time.

This is rather different. There is, as Saintsbury says, no
suggestion of blank verse and "no splith of epithets, not
one of the common rhetorical devices to 'get rhythm' ";
but has it what Saintsbury claims for it, "an unbroken,
unslurred current of harmony right through"? It begins

badly, with too much contrast of long and short phrasing. But the second sentence, "Passages . . . come home to him . . . and pierce him . . . with their sad earnestness and vivid exactness" is a beautiful surprise. It combines the favorite *quasi pizzicato* of Newman with a rounded structure; and the asymmetrical balance of "sad earnestness" and "vivid exactness" is very satisfying at the end. But there is little regularity in the curves here or in the remaining sentences, though several three-beat groups occur, notably

> with all its obvious advantages
> is utterly unable to rival.

There is no blank verse, and even less than in most writers who have an ear for sound, of simple metrical runs, like "yet hope of better things." And on the other side of style, the awkward repetition of "thinks" and the pleonasm of "current literature of his own day" must be scored against Newman.

But once more, and to disavow prejudice, take this from "The Second Spring," written in the same year as my first selection. It makes use of the same large and commonplace metaphor, but it is one of the truest examples of genuine purple in all Newman, and it does rely on the common device to "get rhythm," a careful organization of similar or graduated groups.[1]

We have the familiar experience | of the order, the constancy, the perpetual renovation | of the material world which surrounds us.| Frail and transitory as is every part of it, | restless and migratory as are its elements, | never-ceasing as are its changes, | still it abides.| It is bound together by a law of permanence, | it is set up in unity; | and, though it is ever dying, | it is ever coming to life again. | Dissolution does but give birth to fresh modes of organization, | and one death is the parent of a thousand lives. | Each hour, as it comes, | is but a testimony, | how fleeting, | yet how secure, | how certain, | is the great whole. | It is like an image on the waters, | which is ever the same, | though the waters ever flow. | Change upon change | —yet one change cries out to another, | like the alternate Seraphim, | in praise and in glory of their Maker. | The sun sinks to rise again; | the day is swallowed up in the gloom of the night, | to be reborn out of it, | as fresh as if it had never been quenched.| Spring passes into summer, | and through summer and autumn into winter, | only the more surely, | by its own ultimate return, | to triumph over that grave, | towards which it resolutely hastened from its first hour.| We mourn over the blossoms of May, | because they are to wither; | but we know, withal, | that May is one day to have its revenge upon November, | by the revolution of that solemn circle | which never stops | —which teaches us in our height of hope, | ever to be sober, | and in our depth of desolation, | never to despair.

ii

In a subject as difficult as this of prose rhythm it would be unsafe to miss any opportunity for clearness, even at the risk of a little repetition. And one of the primary distinctions to be made, though I have been a long time coming to it, is that of quantitative and qualitative. Since all prose consists of speech sounds, all prose is potentially rhythmic, whatever one's definition of rhythm may be. But it is plain that, according to the ability or the intention of the writer, some prose will be *more rhythmic* than other prose in the sense that it will have more definite, more marked, more easily recognized rhythms than other prose. From verse, at one end of the scale, there will be successive gradations of less and less, down to a point, not of course a vanishing point, but one at which the rhythms will be hardly noticeable even to

a very attentive ear, or at which the rhythms will be accidental and so to say inorganic. This kind of prose may be
conveniently called a-rhythmic, meaning not that it is
without rhythm but that it does not produce the effect of
conscious or artistic rhythm; in a word, the quantity of
rhythm is at a minimum. This a-rhythmic prose may
be thought of in two ways, either as a class of prose composition in which rhythm is inconspicuous or unimportant,
or as a kind of prose constantly intermingling with that
which is more highly rhythmized. That is, one may
expect a-rhythmic passages or parts even in the prose
which is characterized in the main by conspicuous and significant rhythms. From either point of view the quantity
of rhythm in any one piece will be difficult to measure
because there is no clear objective test; it will always be
relative not only to other pieces or its own context, but
also to the perception of different readers at different
times. In some prose the rhythms are so patent that no
one will be likely to miss them. In other prose, which
will include the very best, the rhythms are perceptible
only to a trained or attentive ear, and often then only
when a sufficient amount of attention is free from the
other obligations of reading.

On the scale of quantitative rhythm, practical prose,
the prose of fact and exposition, will be at one end—a-
rhythmic prose. It should hardly be necessary to offer
examples, but I will give two. The first is from Professor Baldwin's book on Mediæval Rhetoric:

The international affairs of the Roman Curia demanded
and developed professional *notarii*. Their first and abiding
concern was precision. Legal correctness of language, exacti-
tude, systematic verification and record, precaution against
tampering and forgery, all demanded an elaborate technical

skill. This was *ars notaria* in the stricter sense, an important branch of the practise of law, especially of canon law. Beyond legal correctness and dignity it developed style befitting Rome. Privileges, decrees, mandates, dispensations, commissions, and other forms observed exact appropriateness and rhythms were at once marks of authenticity and models. The same care extended to diplomatic correspondence. The documents in both fields, a mine for students of medieval history, amply attest the importance of *dictamen* as a profession.

One reads this without any consciousness of its rhythms; one's attention is wholly on its content; and so no doubt was the author's while writing it. Yet notice the four binary groups in the first and fourth sentences and the four groups of three stresses in the third sentence; notice also the balance of "demanded and developed" and "professional *notarii*," the consecutive anapests of "an elaborate technical skill," the dactyls of "amply attest the importance of," and the iambs of "developed style befitting Rome." These are certainly the materials of rhythm, and they are quite unmistakable; yet one would not say that the paragraph exhibits *rhythm* in any real sense. It does not *flow*, and it is not meant to; it is adequate and serviceable.

For an example of a different sort, take a passage from one of the recognized masters of English prose, writing on a subject which he may be supposed to have understood: the third sentence of Pater's essay on "Style."

Critical efforts to limit art *a priori*, by anticipations regarding the natural incapacity of the material with which this or that artist works, as the sculptor with solid form, or the prose-writer with the ordinary language of men, are always liable to be discredited by the facts of artistic production; and while prose is actually found to be a coloured thing with

Bacon, picturesque with Livy and Carlyle, musical with Cicero
and Newman, mystical and intimate with Plato and Michelet
and Sir Thomas Browne, exalted or florid, it may be, with
Milton and Taylor, it will be useless to protest that it can
be nothing at all, except something very tamely and nar-
rowly confined to mainly practical ends—a kind of "good
round-hand"; as useless as to protest that poetry might not
touch prosaic subjects as with Wordsworth, or an abstruse
matter as with Browning, or treat contemporary life nobly
as with Tennyson.

This contains even fewer of the materials of rhythm
than we observed in the preceding specimen, though the
binary groups at the beginning and the ternary groups at
the close are noticeable; and as a sentence it is not conspicuous for that "all-important" structure which (as
Pater says a little later in the same essay) is "in literary
art as in all other . . . felt, or painfully missed, everywhere." But it is no less a-rythmic than the professor's
paragraph; it does not flow, and it is not meant to flow.

A hundred other examples would only illustrate the
same fact, that it is no derogation from the merits of
good prose to say that it may be a-rhythmic. Bad prose
may be bad in sound as in other respects; but bad prose is
not the present concern. Good prose may be more or
less rhythmical; when it is least rhythmical and yet good
prose we call it a-rhythmic.

The intermixture in the same composition, even in
the same paragraph and in adjacent sentences, of passages
with strongly marked rhythm and passages in which the
rhythm is less remarkable is based of course on the general principle of variation. Prose which is too rhythmic
(the opposite of a-rhythmic) may be good in its way, provided it does not turn into bad verse. Extreme tension

must be varied by periods of relaxation. The cultivated ear is easily wearied by the tom-tom. As in opera aria alternates with recitative, so in prose the finer passages are set off by those pitched in a lower key; and Dryden was only the first to observe that the great flights of *Paradise Lost* had necessarily to be relieved by 'flats.' Yet a certain level must be maintained or the change will appear too abrupt. The rhetoric of Macaulay is to sensitive readers something of a strain, and so is the formality of Gibbon: the rhythms in both are well marked, but they tire. Even the comparatively short *Urn Burial* of Sir Thomas Browne, wonderfully sustained as it is, becomes a little trying if read aloud; and even there one feels the variations with a sense of relief. The paragraph beginning "What song the Syrens sang" does not hold throughout the level at which it commences. But it is with the habitual wearers of the purple that one finds the contrast clearest, in Pater, say, and sometimes Ruskin. I have already remarked upon the sudden drop after the Monna Lisa portrait: the flight is ended, the wings folded, and the reader feels too quickly the hard ground on which he is deposited.

On the other hand, there is an almost perfect illustration of successful descent at the end of section 2 of De Quincey's *The English Mail-Coach*. The climax has been built up steadily through several pages, in De Quincey's most dramatic, elocutionary manner, and the last two paragraphs are:

But the lady——! Oh, heavens! will that spectacle ever depart from my dreams, as she rose and sank upon her seat, sank and rose, threw up her arms wildly to heaven, clutched at some visionary object in the air, fainting, praying, raving, despairing? Figure to yourself, reader, the elements of the

case; suffer me to recall before your mind the circumstances
of that unparalleled situation. From the silence and deep
peace of this saintly summer night—from the pathetic blend-
ing of this sweet moonlight, dawnlight, dreamlight—from
the manly tenderness of this flattering, whispering, murmur-
ing love—suddenly as from the woods and fields—suddenly
as from the chambers of the air opening in revelation—suddenly as from the ground yawning at her feet, leaped upon
her, with the flashing of cataracts, Death the crowned phan-
tom, with all the equipage of his terrors, and the tiger roar
of his voice.

The moments were numbered; the strife finished; the
vision was closed. In the twinkling of an eye, our flying
horses had carried us to the termination of the umbrageous
aisle; at the right angles we wheeled into our former direction; the turn of the road carried the scene out of my eyes
in an instant, and swept it into my dreams for ever.

There was grave risk of disaster in this rather plain
résumé, with its quick change from the poetic to the
expository, from the greater to the lesser rhythms. But
the last sentence is just the right introduction to the
"Dream-Fugue" which immediately follows.

Movement in the other direction is more usual—from
plain to colored, as in this, with its gentle irony:

The poets in the country puzzled and amused me: I would
take them to remote valleys, through flowering orchards
and hanging beech woods, yet they never seemed to notice
anything. Yeats would keep his eyes on the ground, and
while Davies was with us, he would talk literary gossip, and
ask my opinion of this or that poet, while cuckoos sang and
rainbows arched the valley.

Or from rough to smooth, as in this (one of the worst
sentences in English fiction, yet saved from lowest per-
dition by the last dozen words):

He was of Lady Charlotte's mind, in her hot zeal against injustice done to the creatures she despised; and yet more than she applauded a woman who took up her idiot husband's challenge to defend her good name, and cleared it, right or wrong, and beat him down on his knees, and then started for her spell of the merry canter over turf: an example to the English of the punishment they get for their stupid Puritanic tyranny—sure to be followed by a national helter-skelter down-hill headlong.

DeQuincey gives us also a transcendent paragraph in which the variation is so cunningly managed that even a highly artificial passage does not "stick fiery off" but lies unobtrusively in its setting, namely, the roses-and-Fanny sentences, already exhibited, from section 1 of *The English Mail-Coach.*

If, therefore, the crocodile does *not* change, all things else undeniably *do:* even the shadow of the pyramids grows less. And often the restoration in vision of Fanny and the Bath road makes me too pathetically sensible of that truth. Out of the darkness, if I happen to call back the image of Fanny, up rises suddenly from a gulf of forty years a rose in June; or, if I think for an instant of the rose in June, up rises the heavenly face of Fanny. One after the other, like the antiphonies in the choral service, rise Fanny and the rose in June, then back again the rose in June and Fanny. Then come both together, as in a chorus—roses and Fannies, Fannies and roses, without end, thick as blossoms in paradise. Then comes a venerable crocodile, in a royal livery of scarlet and gold, with sixteen capes; and the crocodile is driving four-in-hand from the box of the Bath mail. And suddenly we upon the mail are pulled up by a mighty dial, sculptured with the hours, that mingle with the heavens and the heavenly host. Then, all at once we are arrived in Marlborough forest, amongst the lovely households of the roe-deer: the deer and their fawns retire into the dewy thickets; the thickets are rich with roses; once again the roses call up

the sweet countenance of Fanny; and she, being the grand-
daughter of a crocodile, awakens a dreadful host of semi-
legendary animals—griffins, dragons, basilisks, sphinxes—
till at length the whole vision of fighting images crowds
into one towering armorial shield, a vast emblasonry of
human charities and human loveliness that have perished,
but quartered heraldically with unutterable and demoniac
natures, whilst over all rises, as a surmounting crest, one
fair female head, with the forefinger pointing, in sweet,
sorrowful admonition, upwards to heaven, where is sculptured the eternal writing which proclaims the frailty of earth
and her children.[2]

iii

There have been examples enough already of rhythms
which are too obvious, too regular, and therefore offensive both to the ear and, if one may say so in the hearing
of Dr. Johnson, to the judgment also. Yeats complained
of the "long, flaccid, structureless sentences" in some of
George Moore's most praised work. But this was a cultivated product of Moore's, perhaps most fully displayed
in *The Brook Kerith,* and there described if not defended.
"And as if foreseeing an ardent disciple he began to speak
to Joseph of God, his speech moving on with a gentle
motion like that of clouds wreathing and unwreathing,
finding new shapes for every period, and always beautiful
shapes."

And his thoughts running on incontinently, he imagined
Timothy a prisoner in Jerusalem and himself forced to de-
cide whether he should go there to defend Timothy or
abandon his mission. A terrible choice it would be for him
to have to choose between his duty towards men and his
love of his son, for Timothy was more to him than many
sons are to their fathers, the companion of all his travels and
his hope, for he was falling into years and needed Timothy

now more than ever. But it was not likely that the Jews had heard that Timothy was travelling from Jericho to Cæsarea, and it was a feverish imagination of his to think that they would have time to send out agents to capture Timothy. But if such a thing befell how would he account to Eunice for. . . .

So it runs on, page after page, a kind of murmurous undertone, too lulling. Contrast with it Traherne's *Centuries of Meditations,* which Mr. Read praises as "written in a sweetly modulated rhythm which has no parallel in English prose."

Another time in a lowering and sad evening, being alone in the field, when all things were dead and quiet, a certain want and horror fell upon me, beyond imagination. The unprofitableness and silence of the place dissatisfied me; its wideness terrified me; from the utmost ends of the earth fears surrounded me. How did I know but dangers might suddenly arise from the East, and invade me from the unknown regions beyond the seas? I was a weak and little child, and had forgotten there was a man alive in the earth. Yet something also of hope and expectation comforted me from every border. This taught me that I was concerned in all the world; and that in the remotest borders the causes of peace delight me, and the beauties of the earth when seen were made to entertain me: that I was made to hold a communion with the secrets of Divine Providence in all the world: that a remembrance of all the joys I had from my birth ought always to be with me: that the presence of Cities, Temples, and Kingdoms ought to sustain me, and that to be alone in the world was to be desolate and miserable. The comfort of houses and friends, the clear assurance of treasures everywhere, God's care and love, His goodness, wisdom, and power, His presence and watchfulness in all the ends of the earth, were my strength and assurance for ever: and that these things being absent to my eye, were my joys and consolations, as present to my understanding as the wideness and emptiness of the Universe which I saw before.

The contrast needs no pointing. And still keeping to the seventeenth century, contrast this, where "intelligence and emotion are almost equal forces," with a huddled periodic sentence of Milton's, which you would hardly condemn for want of rhythm but in which feeling and ideas crowd each other faster than grammar can absorb and arrange them.

After our liberty and religion thus prosperously fought for, gained, and many years possessed, except in those unhappy interruptions which God hath removed; now that nothing remains but in all reason the certain hopes of a speedy and immediate settlement for ever in a firm and free Commonwealth, for this extolled and magnified nation, regardless both of honour won or deliverances vouchsafed from Heaven, to fall back, or rather to creep back so poorly, as it seems the multitude would, to their once abjured and detested thraldom of kingship, to be ourselves the slanderers of our own just and religious deed, though done by some to covetous and ambitious ends, yet not, therefore, to be stained with their infamy, or they to asperse the integrity of others; and yet these now by revolting from the conscience of deeds well done, both in church and state, to throw away and forsake, or rather to betray, a just and noble cause for the mixture of bad men who have ill-managed and abused it (which had our fathers done heretofore, and on the same pretence deserted true religion, what had long ere this become of our gospel, and all Protestant reformation so much intermixed with avarice and ambition by some reformers?) and, by thus relapsing, to verify all the bitter predictions of our triumphing enemies, who will now think they wisely discerned and justly censured both us and all our actions as rash, rebellious, hypocritical, and impious,—not only argues a strange, degenerate contagion suddenly spread among us, fitted and prepared for new slavery, but will render us a scorn and derision to all our neighbors.

Thus we come near to a perilous question: can there

be bad rhythms? Are the involved sentences of Henry James, for example—

She would also have, in holidays, to look after the small boy, who had been for a term in school—young as he was to be sent, but what else could be done?—and who, as the holidays were about to begin, would be back from one day to the other.—

always stopping and starting in unexpected ways, filled with curlicues as well as curves, rhythmically bad?[3] Is Saintsbury's perfervid defence of Swift's phrase "only a woman's hair" rhythmically wrong? or not rhythmic at all?

We are all of us sometimes fools (this will hardly be denied by anyone who is not always one). But if any person—no matter how little of a fool at other times or in other ways, no matter how rare his sojourn in the House of Folly may be—if any person has seen, see, or till the Day of Judgment shall see in those four words cynicism, brutality, anything but the expression of the riddle of the painful earth in one of its forms expressed more poignantly and finally than it has been expressed by any uninspired human being excepting Shakespeare—then it is safe, with no flippancy or triumph, but with all the gravity and sadness that the thoughts of life and death can inspire, to pronounce that person—at the point of time and in the actual expression of his thought —not a brute, not a cynic, not anything—but an utter and hopeless fool. (A Saintsbury Miscellany)

We should have an answer to such questions, an answer resting on more than mood or taste. But probably we shall find none. For the ear is independent and unaccountable. Saintsbury quotes a passage from Shaftesbury's Characteristics and tells us that the "last sentence, particularly, is as formless a heap as can be found in mid-seventeenth century, without any of the rhythmical beauty

of parts which so often redeems the prose of that time"
(p. 255).

But what can one do? or how dispense with these darker
disquisitions or moonlight voyages, when we have to deal
with a sort of moon-blind wits who, though very acute and
able in their kind, may be said to renounce daylight, and
extinguish in a manner the bright visible outward world,
by allowing us to know nothing beside what we can prove
by strict and formal demonstration?

Certainly it is a shapeless sentence, loosely straggling,
without the energy and impetus of Milton's or the "sweetness" of Traherne's. But what makes it rhythmically
inferior?

Meredith begins a chapter of *Beauchamp's Career*
thus:

That pure opaque of the line of downs ran luminously
edged against the pearly morning sky, with its dark land-
ward face crepusculine yet clear in every combe, every dotting copse and furze-bush, every wavy fall, and the ripple,
crease, and rill-like descent of the turf. Beauty of darkness
was there, as well as beauty of light above.

This is rather self-conscious and studied; and no one, I
suppose, will find it smooth or easy. At the best it is
rhythmical without being melodious. Nearly half of it
will scan, but the other parts fit ill with metrical runs:
"luminously edged . . . the pearly morning sky." For it
is characteristic of Meredith to intermingle harshness
maliciously, as though to avoid a threat of commonplace
beauty. Mr. Read quotes a paragraph from Doughty's
Arabia Deserta and comments on the deliberately intentional peculiarities of arrangement and emphasis in the
first part; "the rest of the paragraph," he says, "eases its

rhythm to permit a relaxed observation. . . . The re-
tardation of the rhythm, towards the end of the paragraph, until it ends with a sense of inevitability on the
word 'sleep,' is also a deliberate effect" (pp. 41 f.). Here
is the paragraph; let us examine it from our point of view.

Pleasant, as the fiery heat of the desert daylight is done,
is our homely evening fire. The sun gone down upon a
highland steppe of Arabia, whose common altitude is above
three thousand feet, the thin dry air is presently refreshed,
the sand is soon cold; wherein yet at three fingers' depth is
left a sunny warmth of the past day's heat until the new sunrise. After a half hour it is the blue night, and clear hoary
starlight in which there shines the girdle of the milky way,
with a marvellous clarity. As the sun is setting, the nomad
housewife brings in a truss of sticks and dry bushes, which
she has pulled or hoed with a mattock (a tool they have
seldom) in the wilderness; she casts down this provision by
our hearthside, for the sweet-smelling evening fire. But to
Hirfa, his sheykhly young wife, Zeyd had given a little
Beduin maid to help her. The housewife has upon her woman's side an hearth apart, which is the cooking-fire. Commonly Hirfa baked then, under the ashes, a bread-cake for
the stranger: Zeyd her husband, who is miserable, or for
other cause, eats not yet, but only near midnight, as he is
come again from the mejlis and would go in to sleep.

Most persons who are not already accustomed to
Doughty's manner will probably agree that a first reading
of this is not easy. The inversion of the first sentence is
striking, and prepares one for a poetic tone. Then the
dependent clause is almost metrical, with alliteration, and
the sentence ends with three iambs. The next begins with
a blank verse, and ends, or seems to end with the abrupt
"sand is soon cold"—the remainder is what Saintsbury
calls in condemnation epexegetical, but contains in "past

day's heat" an echo of "thin dry air," which in turn sends
one back for echoes which confuse the ear: "three fingers'
depth," "highland steppe," "sunny warmth," "new sunrise." The next sentence however echoes "soon cold"
with "half hour" and "blue night" and "new sunrise"
with "clear hoary" and "highland steppe" with "milky
way"; and the blank verse returns with "there shines the
girdle of the milky way." The next is tuneless and
patchy, until the cadence of "the sweet-smelling evening
fire." The rest is broken in grammar and in rhythm,
thanks partly to the strange words and the overemphatic
"eats not yet," but is softened by the approximate blank
verse of "The housewife has upon her woman's side."
Evidently Mr. Read has found here his own music, which
is not for all ears; but his praise may well remind us of
the indisputable differences of taste. Perhaps we can
agree that Doughty's rhythms are deliberately difficult
and there let the defence rest.

More on this matter of bad rhythm would be hard to
bear, but a final illustration pointing a somewhat different
direction may be permitted.

These are spots in your feasts of charity, when they feast
with you, feeding themselves without fear: clouds they are
without water, carried about of winds; trees whose fruit
withereth, without fruit, twice dead, plucked up by the roots;
raging waves of the sea, foaming out their own shame;
wandering stars, to whom is reserved the blackness of darkness for ever.

"Probably there is not one unpractised reader in ten,"
says Coventry Patmore, "but would feel slightly embar-
rassed by having to read this passage of St. Jude aloud
for the first time. The meaning is nevertheless plain;
the places of all but one or two of the accents are unmis-

takable; so that if stress and tone without measured time were the only points requiring to be given in prose reading, everybody would read it off properly at once. The peculiarity of the passage, however, consists in its singular departure from the metrical constitution of ordinary English phrases, which exhibit a great preponderance of emphatic and unemphatic syllables in consecutive couples, whereas here the accents fall, for the most part, either upon adjacent syllables, or upon every third syllable,— an arrangement requiring an exceedingly bold and emphatic style of delivery, *in order to sever accent from accent by equal measures of time.*" That Patmore was a pronounced 'timer' is obvious enough; and that anyone should regard a prose passage as difficult to read because it is not metrical is surprising enough; yet in his oblique way Patmore has perceived that there is something wrong with the movement of the passage and has all but correctly pointed to the trouble. The members are short, the pauses frequent, the grammar is bare of convenient connectives, and smoothness is sacrificed for abruptness and emphasis. If by equal measures of time he means compensating for the pauses, we have no quarrel with him. But the passage *is* singular in its deliberate avoidance of the simplest means of making it easy to read aloud.

iv

Much as has been written in an effort to analyze our experience of poetry, little of it has gone beyond emphasis on the complex inter-relations of its emotional and intellectual elements together with its 'music,' the sounds of words and lines, singly and in groups: thought and feeling

> Urged by the great rejoicing wind that sings
> With draught of unseen wings.

But at least a general or vague recognition of the power
of sound is seldom omitted, great as may be the difficulty
of separating it from the other components and of weigh-
ing its contributive values. In estimating our experience
of prose, however, the sound is usually taken for granted,
negatively: it is admitted and neglected, with almost
no attempt to analyze it. Yet the sound of prose—artistic or emotive prose, all but the poorest pedestrian
prose—is as certainly a constituent of the total effect as
the meaning is. One may be inattentive to it, but unless
one is deaf, one does not escape it. At the very least it
is an element of the ease or difficulty of apprehension,
and no less than in poetry is it integral with the content.

On the principle of economy, when the words do not
flow there results an obstruction to their meaning. The
attention is distracted, and something is lost. If two ideas
which are not similar, or similar in opposition, are presented in parallel form, the mind is momentarily confused. If one idea is to be balanced against another and
the expression is not also balanced, both in syntax and in
sound, the effect is dissipated. If the construction is
abrupt without a corresponding abruptness in the thought,
if a rhetorical curve is set in motion and its answering
curve does not follow, or if mere words are thrust in
to fill out a vacancy in the rhythm, if a parenthesis in-
terrupts the movement and diverts its flow, or a trailing
epexegesis continues after the music has ceased—whenever the ear is thwarted of its expectation, by too much or
too little, there is a risk of concomitant thwarting of
communication. This is merely the principle of economy,
the functional value of rhythm. Prose creates its own
movement out of itself, and the rhythm is born of the
thought and feeling it brings us. The language which

conveys them contains within it its true rhythm. In this sense rhythm and style are simultaneous and synonymous.

There is also the principle of beauty. As one star differs from another in glory, so one word or arrangement of words may differ from another in the pleasure its sound affords us. So "an art to make dust of all things" pleases more than "a power to reduce everything to dust," just as

> For one restraint, Lords of the world beside

pleases more than "lords of the world except for one limitation." No one would hold that the following sentence is anything but barbarous from any point of view:

Sir A. Pigott, on the other hand, contended, that as his client had written this work merely for his own amusement, without the most distant idea of his children seeing it, it was extremely hard that he should be deprived of the exercise of his parental rights, as the work was a mere effusion of imagination.

It is not so easy to point out what is wrong with this one:

Even today, with our far more numerous organs of criticism, a yearly average of about ten reviews and more than one poem during the whole of his publishing career would be unusual publicity for a poet whose subjects were avowedly unpopular.

But certainly it lacks the functional beauty of properly distributed parts, and the mere sound of it betrays the error. (The incorrect use of "with," the cant "organs of criticism" and "publishing career," and the discord of "publishing," "publicity" are of course obvious.) On the other hand, in this sentence, which has no special distinction of content and no pretense to beauty of form—

There was a string of narrow woods called Plumstead Coppices which ran from a point near the church right across the parish, dividing the archdeacon's land from the Ullathorne estate, and these coppices, or belts of woodland, belonged to the archdeacon.—

the easy, quiet movement, following a true course to its point at the end, is gratifying to the ear. And to go a step higher: here the thought is well matched with a beauty of sound—

In hope of honours, lulled by flowing wave around their aisles of sacred sand, each with his name written and the cross graved at his side, lay her dead.

v

A recent work on linguistic science divides the description of language into three parts: grammar, lexicography, and stylistic, and explains the last in these words:

Stylistic treats of the selection among linguistic responses possible in a given situation. It shows how one man will use certain words and syntactic constructions where another man will employ a more or less different linguistic medium. It also shows that different situations call for different words and phrases quite aside from the obvious requirements of meaning. (Sturtevant, p. 52)

This, though not so intended, is a curiously informal description of what we mean by *style:* the selection in accordance with individual habit and judgment of certain words and arrangements of words to fit the particular requirements of communication. But it omits the element of pleasingness which usually distinguishes one selection from another—a pleasingness of which the principal criterion is sound, movement, rhythm. When the lexical and grammatical necessities are satisfied, the rest is style: "the gesture of the mind and of the soul." My Lord Chancellor, Sir Francis Bacon, liked his music sharp and loud: "I ever loved easy airs that go full, all the parts together; and not those strange points of accord and discord": and so he wrote in the *Essays*, with a few exceptions. But in the *Advancement* he revealed his enjoyment of many strange points. Some people are like Fielding's Partridge: they admire a style that anybody can see is a style: among whom are the *stylists*, R. L. S., for example, and Pater (who almost deserves George Moore's quip that in his books the English language lies in state), and Ruskin. But Ruskin more than any of them commanded the whole range of styles, from pedestrian, for exposition; to plain, which does its work adequately; to poetic, in which the Muses take part; to flamboyant, in which he soared for the mere joy of using his wings; and in each of them, though he may not have mingled them judiciously, there is its own rhythm not so much fitted to as naturally fitting its purpose and content. There is a paragraph in the second volume of *Modern Painters* which he described, thirty-seven years after its first publication, as "one of the most valuable in essential contents I have ever written, but the literary art and pedantry of it [he added,] employed to express the most solemn of truths in a tinkle that shall be pleasant to the ear, are now very grievous to me." Thus the gestures may alter with time, for in 1846 Ruskin was confessedly writing in imitation of Hooker. But the fault was in choice of model for the purpose, not in success of imitation: he should not have soared with sixteenth-century wings.

But there is never any need to claim too much. In general, prose which we regard as excellent in other respects, as really excellent, is likely to excel in rhythm also. The fine passages gathered up by Saintsbury and the *Oxford Book of English Prose* and similar collections are notable for other qualities than rhythm. And this is as it should be. For rhythm does not exist by itself, alone, but as an integral part of the potential beauty and power of prose, as a function (in the mathematical sense) of the other expressive elements of language. When it is isolated for purposes of exposition and analysis, there is danger of giving it a false emphasis, which is, however, easily corrected. Those who have been content to leave it, neglected, as one of the unapproachable mysteries, and even like Peter to deny it while they still believe, or who have narrowed it by puristic definition almost out of existence, must be met with reciprocal patience until mutual faith is renewed. To exclude from the province of prose rhythm all but successions of equal intervals of time, to pass over the other characteristics which make prose a moving, flowing series of irregular yet echoing and responsive parts, is merely to reject one of the important sources of beauty and strength, one of the principal resources of affective language for the sake of a theoretic concept. If 'rhythm' is the wrong word, let us by all means look for a better one, but not sacrifice the pleasure of seeing and feeling the substance because we cannot come to terms with the shadow.

VIII

Conclusion—Primer

i

THERE ARE THOSE who worship at home, or in
the forest, or in the open field. But there are others
who can find the god only in his temple; and the approach
to his temple may be a long series of arduous steps. For
some it is inspiration and afflatus, for others it is ritual.
The world has room for both. For atheists and agnostics,
too, there is a little room set aside, in which they may
practise their antiworship. "Wir sprachen über Rhythmus
im allgemeinen," said Goethe to Eckermann, "und kamen
darin überein, dass sich über solche Dinge nicht denken
lassen." And Mr. Edgerton Smith, author of an excellent book on versification, tells us that rhythm in prose,
or even "a rhythmical tendency," is "in a passage of any
considerable length, usually no more than a tendency
and is quite unobtrusive, only to be found when we look
for it, and even then only by some straining." On the
other hand: "—Rhythm—said Stephen [who was then
the artist as young man]—is the first formal esthetic relation of part to part in any esthetic whole or of an esthetic
whole to its part or parts or to any part of the esthetic
whole of which it is a part."

ii

As the common reader of poetry is content to take
prosody for granted—like sunshine and flowers, and some-

times rain: provisions of an inscrutable but somehow kindly providence—so the common reader of prose is content to take the rhythm of language as a natural growth, or as an 'accompaniment.' There are said to be people for whom music is a tune, and all the rest the accompaniment, a vague addition acceptable but unnecessary. But the impatience which resists analysis is its own reward.

It is the function of analysis to examine into the unapparent, to discover the hidden springs and sources, to find and chart the undercurrents. To suppose that a writer deliberately contrives all his effects, in prose or in verse, would not only be absurd, it would deny the undeniable mystery which broods over all the processes of affective expression in language. From a simple statement of fact to the most elaborate evocation of mood, there is in all our speech an element of the unknown, the unexpected, something which is not the result of taking thought. It ranges all the way from the commonplace of habit to the strange working of the unconscious which is callen inspiration. It is true that analysis may in its weaker moments bring up from the deep mysteries which have no existence outside of an ingenious imagination; but that is a danger we have to face, for the test of probability is prejudgment. Therefore a willing suspension of reason, and even a little credulousness, must go with us until all the ways are made plain and all the mysteries revealed—which will not be soon.

The deliberate contrivances of professional skill and concealed art, however, are not to be underestimated. Some writers reveal too much; they are guildsmen and have their mark by which we know them. We see their intention, be it artful simplicity or intricate nodosity; and when they are marking time we hear the beat without the music. We are amused but not deceived by their prestidigitation. It is then the business of analysis to discover and display both what the writer deliberately, with all the resources of his art, puts into his prose—his prose rhythm, for our present concern—and what by the processes of composition, mysterious even to him, is added thereto from the overworld of his trained or inspired gift. It is not fair to object, therefore, that the author could not have intended all these curiosities of rhythm and for that reason they have no existence except in the vain imaginings of an analyst. Many such subtleties are no doubt intentional and others just as certainly the product of other than conscious workings of the mind. What produces them is not our concern now; to find them out and point them out is enough for the present.

For both writer and reader it is largely a matter of attention, this watching and catching the unexpected melodies and the deeper richer volume of sound which accompanies them. Said Herbert Spencer, shrewdly, thinking of the reader only: "The more time and attention it takes to receive and understand each sentence, the less time and attention can be given to the contained idea." How much time and attention are then left for the sound of the sentences? Hence the threefold effort, the triple strain, both in writing and in reading, required of us if we are to distinguish and follow the interweavings of the fugal voices. Hence also the richness of the fabric.

But there is also the danger of overemphasis, the unbalance of the three voices, when syntax or sense or sound dominates, one over the others, in prejudice or in conflict. And the moment we begin to read, we at once cross the writer's interests with our own, particularly our

mental habits and more particularly our rhythmic pre-
occupations, and then the attempt to arrive at any valid
objective judgment becomes really difficult. One thing
we can do, however, is to try to *over*hear the movement
in our own language and to study it in the language of
others; to read with very special attention to the sound,
making nevertheless due allowance for the exaggeration
which this special attention will entail. Thus can latent
or concealed rhythms be discovered. Then, when the necessary overemphasis has served its purpose, it can be reduced or discarded, and the rhythms felt in their normal
fashion. Any analytical exposition focuses undue attention on details, but the necessary readjustment can easily
be made and the proper perspective attained.

To explain, to explicate, is to unfold, to lay the matter
out flat, so that it can be seen all at once; to reduce three
dimensions to two; and in the process something is lost.
But rhythm is more than an aggregate of parts or syn-
thesis of elements; it is a four-dimensional complex requiring for its apprehension special knowledge and a kind
of imagination. So, after the patient analysis or taking
apart there must be a reassembling which can only be
accomplished by intuitive understanding.

iii

What more? Between the negative extreme which
denies the fact of prose rhythm and the other extreme
in which there is too much of what is too obviously
rhythm—prose encroaching on the rights of verse—there
is always the midland or temperate zone. This midland
is occupied by a prose which moves easily and flows
smoothly, one does not always know why, and is appre-
ciated for the economy of effort in following what it says

and for the quiet pleasure of hearing it. It is neither too regular nor too rough. It has a kind of rhythm, albeit a kind of rhythm which fits no formal definition and which almost forbids analysis. One is hardly aware of its being rhythm, and like other good things which are taken for granted, it is sometimes overlooked. Such prose is said to be natural or effortless, either because it does not betray effort or artifice, or simply because the art is well concealed. It is perhaps our best English prose, and of course it is very rare.

There is also in this midland, somewhat southerly, a kind of prose which takes a noble delight in letting its arts shine clear. Nothing really worth doing, it would claim, is ever done without effort; why then should the effort be hidden or disguised? Let it be freely shown and readily recognized, but with modesty and without ostentation. Something of this is implied in Mr. Somerset Maugham's dictum that "prose is a rococo art," though it is not so certain that "the best prose was written when rococo, with its elegance and moderation, attained its greatest excellence." Here at any rate the curves and balance of curves and flowing lines exhibit a palpable rhythm, subdued by decorum yet signaled by conscious elegance.

Then as one moves farther south, there are increasing signs of luxuriance. The colors are brighter, the vegetation thicker, and everything is or seems larger. The vigor of its growth assumes the form of grandeur or the appearance of grandeur. The rhythms of this prose are noticeable, even flamboyant. They draw attention to themselves and may often become oppressive. The most cursory reader feels them, and what is more sees them.

In short, prose is of many kinds, of many good kinds,

and so therefore are its rhythms. Plain prose will have plain rhythms. Even the plainest, like the human beings who produce it, has some character of beauty and some beauty of rhythm. Ornate prose is for ornate matter, and if the subject is poetical, the rhythms will be poetical. When we remember that poetry turns to meter as one method of rendering us susceptible to its thought and feeling, we may well ask: why should prose be denied this advantage? The answer is, of course: it is not. As verse is continually yielding to the attractions of prose, foiling the metronome and by subtle variations subduing the regular throb of its pulse, so prose, when its emotion is heightened, continually approaches, and with right, the regularity of verse. Prose without apparent rhythm is realism; with it, art. The business of the writer is therefore not to make his prose rhythmical, but to find the right rhythms; and it should be the business of the reader to discover and recognize them.

Saintsbury praises Southey's prose for its "adjustment of cadence and symphony to matter, in such proportion and fashion that you never feel the want of rhythmical and sonorous quality, but at the same time are rarely tempted to concentrate your attention on this" (p. 287). This means that Southey's rhythms are felt to be adequate without being noticeable. Such no doubt is our best English prose; such certainly is one of the best kinds of our English prose. Still, for exegetical and exemplary purposes the special and exaggerated are necessary, and one is grateful for them—on two counts. They have their own place and usually their justification, and they teach us by their open play both the faults and dangers of their method and also the intricacies of their complex manipulation.

The last word, however, must be that rhythm comes from within. "We cannot apprehend a work of literature," says Mr. Middleton Murry, "except as a manifestation of the soul of the man who created it." What he creates is a revelation of his own rhythm, declared to us in the language which brings us the contents of his mind; and in whatever small ways we try to analyze and understand his language, we find—if he is a good workman—his own peculiar rhythm manifested there, the rhythm of his soul. It may be superficial or recondite, simple and pure or elaborate to an extreme: it is still a mirror of himself. Our narrower definitions of rhythm as measure and recurrent measure, ebb and flow, flux and reflux, are but echoes of our limited means of searching out the arcane. The soul is never exposed to our immediate scrutiny. We are obliged to study its manifestations in a series of graded stages or progressions, descending from the unknowable to the known, and in an author's prose rhythm, as in a poet's verse, however minutely and pedantically we study it, we have an approach, a small entrance, to the mystery. As Plato said: a good man has good rhythms. A good prose has good rhythms, if we know how to discern them.

iv

The best summing up will be a kind of Primer. Thus—

Rhythm is, by definition, a series, or the effect of a series, of equal, or approximately equal, or seemingly equal, events in time.

The English language has the following acoustical characteristics which are in varying degree determinants in the rhythm of speech: duration or length of syllables;

stress or accent or emphasis; pitch; and to these must be added the effects of tempo and the negative element of pause or silence.

In speech the duration or length of syllables varies, according to the acoustic elements of the syllables and according to the training and habits of the speaker and the subject or content of the words spoken. In English there are no conventions, as in classical prosody, to fix or determine syllabic length. Some syllables are long 'by nature' but may be shortened by the requirements of their context; and syllables which are short 'by nature' may be similarly lengthened.

English verse is the result of an adjustment of the acoustical characteristics of the language to the definite or predetermined metrical pattern. The rhythm of English verse is thus a resultant of the prose rhythm of the sentences and the requirements of one or another of the set patterns.

The events in time, according to the definition, are signaled or marked off by stress or emphasis.

In verse these events are single units (commonly called feet); in prose they are more likely to be composite: groups of two or more emphases united in grammatical or syntactical combinations; or in larger groups determined by the content. These latter are called stress groups. Pitch, though an absolute or independent characteristic of speech-sound, is for the purpose of analyzing speech rhythm to be regarded as a function or form of stress or emphasis. (This is a point of contention among theorists, but attempts at analysis from any other point of view tend to fall under their own weight.)

For the study of prose, the concept of rhythm may be properly extended beyond its strict definition to include its etymological meaning of 'flow'—the ebb and flow of sounds, the alternation and balance of ideas or feelings or syntactical arrangements. In this sense the element of time and equal intervals is subordinated to other considerations and may appear to be almost negligible.

This kind of rhythm is often called the rhythm of the flowing line.

In English prose, rhythm, strictly so called, is usually intermittent; otherwise the events would appear with such regularity as to confuse or destroy the distinction between prose and verse.

The primary rhythm of prose is determined by rhetorical emphases (as distinguished from the conventional or appointed stresses of meter) and is marked by grammatical groups (phrase, clause, sentence, paragraph) with their pauses.

There is also a secondary rhythm which is due partly to the natural alternations of stress and unstress in English speech and partly to our habitual expectation of regularity (as in verse), especially in formal or affective prose. This secondary rhythm appears as latent, half-submerged meter, that is, the sequences of more or less recognizable metrical feet.

This primary rhythm might be called thought-rhythm and the other sound-rhythm; but the two are separate only in the abstract. They constantly overlap, combine, and interweave in a kind of horizontal harmony and counterpoint. One recognizes them separately only for analysis.

In verse, of course, the metrical predominates and is varied by the prose rhythm. In prose the grammatical or rhetorical predominates and may sometimes be enhanced by suggestions of metrical regularity. When neither appears in recognizable form, the language may be said to be a-rhythmic.

But however we measure and subdivide and count, rhythm is not merely an incremental beauty of language but a signature of the writer's integrity and a true echo of his meaning.

Notes

CHAPTER I

1. For a general statement of both aspects, a little confused perhaps, see T. L. Bolton.
2. See, for example, Wolfgang Köhler, chap. v. and chap. vi.
3. Brown, "Time in English Verse Rhythm," p. 75.
4. MacDougall, "Rhythm, Time and Number," p. 93.
5. Lotspeich, p. 296.

CHAPTER II

1. More properly one should add to these volume "and probably bright-ness." Cf. Ogden, "The Attributes of Sound." But neither volume nor brightness of sound is a primary factor of language rhythm.
2. The technical definition of a syllable is full of difficulties. See, for example, Graff (pp. 53 ff.) and also Jones, p. 54: "In theory a syllable consists of a sequence of sounds containing one peak of prominence. In practice it is often impossible to define the limits of a syllable because there is no means of fixing any exact points of minimum prominence." Cf. also Classe, chap. i, who makes a distinction between the grammatical syllable and the rhythmic syllable. His conclusion is: "Considered from the point of view of rhythm, a syllable may be said to be limited by two successive stress-points in the flow of speech. It is *mainly* a subjective notion which seems to depend more on motor factors than on auditory ones. But there is no doubt that it is a phonetic reality, and syllables are measurable on tracings" (p. 45).
3. Compare for example the diminishing length in the following series: *beads—beam—beef—beak; lose—loom—loose—loop; forge—form—forth —fault.* Cf. Fuhrken, pp. 78-81, and Swadesh, pp. 137 ff. and the references there given. A very careful study of syllabic length is to be found in Classe, chap. iii; his summing-up is this: "what we have learned so far —namely, that, everything else being equal, the length of a syllable depends on the nature of the vowel it contains, the number of consonants that follow that vowel, their nature, their grouping; and that, everything else being equal, the length of a syllable is greater if it is closely connected with the preceding [syllable], than if the grammatical link is with the following one" (p. 116).
4. MacColl, p. 43.
5. Griffith, p. 5. The figures represent fifths of a second.
6. Thomson, p. 414. The fractions represent proportions or relative length only.

7. Patterson, p. 63.

8. Eleven of Miss Griffith's eighteen readers paused after "-scape"; seven of them paused after "dreams," where B recognizes no pause.

9. Additional evidence of this sort may be unnecessary, but here are two examples from Miss Griffith's laboratory, in which the range of variation is often striking:

Set	it	for	a	mo	ment	be	side	one	of	those	white	Greek
1.	.72	1.05	.4	1.2	.8	.5	1.3	.85	.65	.88	1.93	1.5
1.3	.8	1.2	.8	1.3	.5	.6	.7	.7	.5	.6	1.7	1.3
1.7	.9	1.	.5	1.7	.9	.5	1.	.8	.5	1.4	1.7	1.4

god	dess	es	or	beau	ti	ful	wo	men	of	an	ti	qui	ty
1.4	.8	1.2	.8	1.	.36	.85	1.	.36	.45	.8	1.56	.26	1.67
.4	.5	.8	.5	.9	.5	.7	.6	.5	.8	1.	1.1	.6	1.2
1.2	1.	1.2	.9	1.	.5	1.3	.8	.6	.7	.7	1.4	.5	1.4

In	the	wind	less	wea	ther	all	seemed	to	be	list	ning	to	the
1.1	.7	2.1	1.4	1.6	1.3	1.6	1.9	.9	1.2	1.7	1.3	.6	.9
1.5	.67	1.15	1.5	.9	.8	1.9	2.	.6	.7	1.3	1.85	.9	.85
.7	.7	1.4	1.3	.9	1.	1.8	1.85	.3	.8	1.2	.9	.4	.65
.6	.5	1.7	1.3	1.	1.1	1.3	1.9	.3	.8	1.4	1.1	.3	.7
1.	.5	1.6	1.3	1.	1.7	2.	1.3	.6	.8	1.65	1.55	.6	.84

roar	of	the	im	me	mo	ri	al	wa	ter	fall
2.3	.8	1.2	.9	1.	1.06	.3	.5	.8	.8	2.1
3.	.5	.45	.84	.46	1.7	.7	.8	1.	.57	3.1
2.1	.6	.8	.7	.3	1.2	.4	.9	.9	.4	1.7
1.9	.5	.8	.7	.4	1.8	.3	.3	.8	.7	1.7
2.45	.4	.7	1.3	.6	1.4	.4	.7	1.2	.65	3.

10. Miss Griffith's tests (p. 25) show that her readers did not pause at 10.59 per cent of the punctuation marks, and 22.93 per cent of their pauses were independent of punctuation.

11. "In the investigation of the effect on rhythm of variations in the duration of sounds, I did not find so much agreement between different individuals as in the case of variations in intensity" (Woodrow, *A Quantitative Study of Rhythm*, p. 38).

12. "Stress may be defined as an impulse (primarily of a psychological nature) which expresses itself in the first place by an increase of pressure in the speech-canal and approximately coincides with the point of greatest pressure" (Classe, p. 37). "All, or any one, or any combination, of the following features may be present [in stress]:

(a) change of auditory intensity or loudness (usually increase),
(b) change of duration or quantity,
(c) change of direction in melodic curve,
(d) change of characteristics of consonants and vowels,
(e) increased amplitude of physiological movements, . . . etc." (*ibid.*, p. 13).

13. E. A. Sonnenschein, p. 57 n. 1. It is only fair to say however that he adds immediately: "But the points are not necessarily marked by an accent or stress of the voice"—which seems to me an excess of caution, necessary perhaps in a theorist. In the rhythm of speech this point coincides so consistently with word accent or rhetorical stress that for practical purposes it is absurd to reject the convenience of regarding stress as the mark of division between groups. Later it will be convenient to associate with the stress rhythmically the syllables which belong with it logically.—For the possible union, or confusion, of stress and pitch, see below.

14. Woodrow, p. 39.

15. An interesting exposition of the melodies resulting from vowel pitch may be read in Henry Lanz, *The Physical Basis of Rime,* chap. ii; but no application is there made to the problems of rhythm.

16. Cf. Woodrow, "The Rôle of Pitch in Rhythm," pp. 54-77, who concludes: "Pitch, intensity and duration can no longer be looked upon as *stellvertretende* factors, any one of which may be substituted for either of the other two. The rôle of each in rhythm is radically different. Intensity has a group-beginning effect: duration a group-ending effect: pitch neither a group-ending nor a group-beginning effect" (p. 77). Such findings have, of course, little application to language rhythm. Cf. further the guarded statement of Classe (p. 3): "I am unable to agree that the melody of speech is an integral part of its rhythm, for it is separable. No one would deny that both factors are intimately connected, but it does not follow that they are one and the same thing, or even different aspects of the same thing. . . . Rhythm is the backbone of melody, the framework on which it hangs. It follows that, whereas one might not perhaps be justified in studying melody quite apart from rhythm, the reverse is not true."

17. The article, for example, by Joseph Tiffin, "Applications of Pitch and Intensity Measurements of Connected Speech," yields but little. In his transcription of Julia Marlowe's reading of the Quality of Mercy speech (p. 229) I find nothing which suggests or resembles parallel curves; and much the same is true of his other experiments.

18. F. N. Scott, "The Scansion of Prose Rhythm."—At a meeting of the Modern Language Association, December 1930, Professors J. Hubert Scott and Zilpha E. Chandler presented a paper (orally; a mimeographed pamphlet was given out) on "The Inflectional Basis of Speech Rhythm," which appears, from the pamphlet, to rely mainly on pitch, though time and stress are included.

19. *Journal of the American Statistical Association,* vi (1935), 150.

20. *Journal of the American Statistical Association,* vi (1935), 266. On the change of intonation accompanying stress, cf. also Classe, p. 37 n. 1 and the account of Lermoyez's experiment.

21. Schubiger, *The Role of Intonation in Spoken English,* pp. 3-4. This little book is a valuable reminder of the functional importance of intonation which we are all too prone to take for granted without analysis. See her bibliography; also Schmidt.

22. Real progress is being made in the analysis of pitch and stress, notably by Kenneth L: Pike, *The Intonation of American Speech,* Ann Arbor, 1946. The scope of this work goes much beyond the above elementary presentation, but while its findings illuminate many of the difficulties and open up promising new directions, it does not contribute a great deal to our general conclusions. With it should be consulted the long review by R. S. Wells, *Language,* XXIII (1947), 255-273, and a shorter review by R. H. Stetson, *International Journal of American Linguistics,* XIII (1947), 189-193. The latter contains this interesting observation: "The measure [in the musical sense] has no place in speech; the free rhythm of speech both in verse and prose is constituted not of like intervals in time, but of LIKE MOVEMENTS whose durations may vary by 50%" (p. 192). See also Heffner, and the review in *Language,* XXVII (1951), 344-62.

CHAPTER III

1. Of the mechanically balanced sentence Saintsbury says well: "The fault is almost as obvious as its merit" (p. 460); and of the Euphuistic manner: "the everlasting see-saw of antithetic balance almost inevitably spoils the rhythm which it is intended to provide" (p. 121). See his admirable comments on Johnson's balance and parallelism, pp. 268 ff.

2. For a long series, see Psalm 29 and Hebrews 11.

3. Mr. Read remarks: "The rhythm of this passage is controlled by the subtle distinction in value made between the colon and semi-colon. The semi-colon seems to mark a carrying over of an even beat; the colon, the recovery of an initial emphasis" (p. 50).

4. For a fuller analysis of parallelism, balance, and antithesis (together with some derogatory remarks on prose rhythm), see W. K. Wimsatt, Jr.

5. "Rhythm . . . is an affair of the paragraph and rhythmically the sentence is subordinated to the paragraph" (Read, p. 51).

6. I have quoted from the American edition, which was printed however in Great Britain. Mr. Read, using another edition with different pagination, prints as one long paragraph what constitutes two paragraphs in my copy. The additional description follows the changing point of view as the boat moves up the river.

7. My analysis, counting stresses, shows the following longer groups: 21, 14, 11, 13, 7, 11, 3, 13, 18. But though there are two elevens and two thirteens, *my* ear at least detects no repetition of time intervals and no "waves" of sound.

8. I am not concerned to quarrel with Mr. Read. His idea of rhythm is in fact so different from mine that it is perhaps even unfair to use him as a point of departure. In his Introduction he implies that rhythm is what gives *life* to words; later he speaks of living and dead paragraphs, and in the former, he says, tropically, "the words rise like clay on the potter's wheel: the downward force of attention, or concentration, or intuition, and the driving force of emotion or feeling—between these forces the words rise up, take shape, become a complete pattern" (p. 66). Doubtless so; but how is one to know when this takes place? Again he says: "*rhythm* is the accent of expression and its accompaniment" (p. 175).

9. Part II, sec. 1, chap. vii, §§5 *et. sqq.* Now to be read in the Library Edition of Ruskin, III, 253 ff.

CHAPTER IV

1. Elton, p. 156.

2. *Chaucer and His Poetry*—last page: "the tragic face behind the satyr's mask." Professor Garrod has a good one in a printed lecture on Arnold; and I heard two in a lecture read in 1947 by Professor Tinker.

3. The first is from Ingersoll's speech "At His Brother's Grave"; the second from a story by Thompson-Seton and was quoted as "sham prose" in *Atlantic Monthly*, XC (1902), 283.

4. Edmund Gurney, *Tertium Quid.* This is sometimes attributed to Archbishop Whately.

5. Swift's deliberate use of metrical prose for humorous effect has been pointed out by A. Sanford Limouze.

6. For this classification cf. MacColl, p. 50; Elton, p. 159. Saintsbury, pp. 342 ff., making the same distinctions, calls them: non-prosaic rhythm or poetry, hybrid verse-prose, pure prose highly rhythmed, prose in general.

7. It is probably true that the language is *naturally* rhythmical because its speakers have rhythmical tendencies in themselves and have impressed those tendencies upon their medium of expression. Something of this may be seen in the preference of many phrases for one particular form, as "butter and eggs," not "eggs and butter," etc. Cf. Tyndall's: "Rhythm is the rule of Nature."

8. Pp. 434, 435 n. 1.

9. See below, on the *cursus.*

10. Quoted in Malcolm Elwin, *Victorian Wallflowers*, London, 1934, p. 279.

11. Cf. J. E. W. Wallin, "Researches on the Rhythm of Speech." The subjects spoke 20 per cent more syllables of prose than of verse per second, and 10 per cent more in an expiration.

12. Work of this type has been done in America by A. Lipsky. Scanning 1000-word passages from various prose writers, Lipsky (pp. 10-12) found the average number of examples of adjacent stresses (i.e., no syllable between stresses) to be 22.68 (ranging from 52.54 in Ruskin's *Modern Painters* to 8.56 in Johnson's essay on Shakespeare), and the same in the Prologue of Tennyson's *The Princess;* of one syllable between stresses 98.52 (ranging from 141.29 in Ruskin to 51.45 in Spencer's *Principles of Psychology)* and 286.52 in Tennyson; of two syllables between stresses 98.95 (ranging from 116.99 in James's *Principles of Psychology* to 75.04 in Spencer) and 28.72 in Tennyson; of three, 65.01 (ranging from 85.44 in Stevenson to 54.30 in Barrie) and 65.01 in Tennyson; of four, 27.53 and 6.04 in Tennyson; of five, 8.80; of six, 2.11. But it is not clear just what conclusions can be drawn from these figures and some of them are, in my judgment, suspicious. Later, scanning passages of *ca.* 400 words and counting groups of two or more successive feet, he found in Stevenson 26 per cent dissyllabic and 5 per cent trisyllabic; in Ruskin 22 per cent and 4 per cent; in Barrie 18 per cent and 12 per cent; in Cooper 8 per cent and 13.5 per cent.

Similar examination of Raleigh's apostrophe to Death, Donne's "If some king of the earth" (quoted at length below, p. 84), Sir Thomas Browne's "What song the syrens sang" (the whole paragraph), and short passages of 300-500 syllables from Bishop Burnet, Jeffrey, Hallam, Ruskin, Shaw's Preface to *Back to Methusaleh,* and a leading article from the *T.L.S.* (1 August 1936), together with fifty lines from *Paradise Lost,* Book I, Wordsworth's Tintern Abbey "Lines" and Byron's *Don Juan,* canto iii, scanned in the same manner, i.e., as prose not as verse, gives the following percentages of unstressed syllables: Raleigh 54.8; Ruskin 61; Donne 61.7; Burnet 62.35; Hallam 62.7; Browne 65.6; Jeffrey 68.8; *T.L.S.* 69.46; Shaw 71.87; and Milton 58.4; Wordsworth 60.2; Byron 60.5. Not a great deal can be inferred from such limited statistics, but subject to correction from a fuller study one or two observations can be made. The theoretical figure for iambic verse would be 50 per cent of stressed and 50 per cent of unstressed syllables. The rather high percentage of unstressed syllables when the sentences are read as prose gives a rough indication of the number of secondary stresses which must be emphasized *metri gratia*. The low percentage of Raleigh is significant and is what one would expect. The closeness of the Donne and Ruskin to the percentage of verse is not surprising, nor perhaps that of Hallam and Burnet, though I had noted them before actually scanning them as more rapid than the others. But the much higher percentage of Jeffrey and Shaw and the *T.L.S.* leader are clearly indicative of the swifter and more characteristic movement of direct non-numerous English prose.

13. The striking difference between these figures and those of Professor Croll is due chiefly to the latitude of his extension of the formulas. As a special check I have scanned all the cadences of the Sunday Collects in the 1558 Prayer Book and made deductions for the frequent repetition of the formulas *Jesus Christ* and *Christ our Lord*—although in estimating the aural influence they ought surely to be considered. The result is 72.5 per cent of nonmedieval cadences, or 27.5 per cent corresponding to the *cursus* forms and their several extensions. The proportion of 5-2 and 6-2 together is about 18 per cent—which is slightly higher than in my incomplete scansions for the 'collection.'

For the more curious I add the following bibliography: Albert C. Clark, "Zielinski's *Clauselgesetz*," *Classical Review*, XIX (1905), 164-172; ———, *Fontes Prosae Numerosae*, Oxford, 1909; ———, *The Cursus in Medieval and Vulgar Latin*, Oxford, 1910; John Shelly, "Rhythmical Prose in Latin and English," *Church Quarterly Review*, LXXIV (1912), 81-98; P. Fijn van Draat, "Rhythm in English Prose," *Anglia*, XXXVI (1912), 1-58; Albert C. Clark, *Prose Rhythm in English*, Oxford, 1913; Oliver Elton, "English Prose Numbers," *Essays and Studies*, IV, 29-54, Oxford, 1913 (reprinted with revisions in *A Sheaf of Papers*, London, 1922); P. Fijn van Draat, "The Cursus in Old English Poetry," *Anglia*, XXXVIII (1914), 377-404; ———, "Voluptas Aurium," *Englische Studien*, XLVIII (1914-15), 394-438; Reginald L. Poole, *Lectures on the History of the Papal Chancery*, Cambridge, 1915, IV, "The Ars Dictandi," pp. 76-97; Finley M. K. Foster, "Cadence in English Prose," *Journal of English and Germanic Philology*, XVI (1917), 456-62; Morris W. Croll, "The Cadence in English Oratorical Prose," *Studies in Philology*, XVI (1919), 1-55; Norton R. Tempest, "Rhythm in the Prose of Sir Thomas Browne," *Review of English Studies*, III (1927), 308-18; Charles S. Baldwin, *Medieval Rhetoric and Poetic*, New York, 1928, pp 223-27; Norton R. Tempest, *The Rhythm of English Prose*, Cambridge, 1930, chap. iii; N. Denholm-Young, "The Cursus in England," *Oxford Essays in Medieval History presented to Herbert Edward Salter*, Oxford, 1934, pp. 68-103. Cf. also Margaret Schlauch, "Chaucer's Prose Rhythms," *PMLA*, LXV (June 1950), 568-89.

CHAPTER V

1. The natural physical necessity of inhalation (since in English as in most languages the speech sounds are produced by the expulsion of the breath) may require a suspension of breath where no grammatical or

rhetorical pause is called for; and this simple fact has led some students to use the term 'breath group.' But it would seem, both from the observation of one's own practice and from the experiments of the laboratory, that generally a reader, or speaker, will manage his breathing to conform with the syntactical divisions of a sentence; and therefore breath groups, while they certainly exist, are not a determinant of speech rhythm. From the other point of view, that of sentences in the course of formation, there is also a tendency to grouping, which according to the Gestalt psychology (Köhler, p. 157) takes place "in the sensory processes": "the equal and similar tend to form units separated from what is dissimilar to them."

2. Such pauses must be recognized as existing, but they may be neglected in any analysis except the most minute. They are of course one of the unstable elements which trouble all analysis.

3. For some readers there may be a little violence in separating the verb "heap" from its object. In fact my first attempt to analyze the clause was: "for in so doing | thou shalt heap coals of fire | on his head" —1 + 3 + 1. But there is surely less emphasis on "heap" than on "coals" and "fire," and this tends to throw the last six words together into one group. Still a different grouping, if the alliteration of *h* is to be brought out, is: "thou shalt heap | coals of fire | on his head"— 1 + 2 + 1; but this seems to me least likely.

4. See note on isochronism, pp. 115 ff.

5. Cf. Miss Griffith's records (p. 49) of "one of those white Greek goddesses | or beautiful women of antiquity." Each member has three stresses; the first has eight syllables, the second has eleven. One of her readers gave 9.21 (fifths of a second) to the first and 9.4 to the second; another gave 9.4 to the first and 9.3 to the second. A third reader, however, showed considerable difference: 6.2 for the first and 9.3 for the second. An even greater difference is recorded for "till it almost stood still | on June afternoons": 10.05 for the first member, 3.6 for the second— whereas the method of counting stresses would make the two roughly equal. (I submit these figures, without prejudice, for what they may signify.)

6. Special students of rhythm sometimes distinguish between logical groups, temporal groups, and experience groups—no doubt properly for their special purposes. Here I prefer to take the logical groups (the words united by their meaning or content, showing in the syntactical arrangements) as the basis and to consider them according to their temporal values, these values being roughly measured by the stresses. An experience group, as I understand it, consists of that part of a sentence perceived or experienced as a unit; it may thus be a combination of logical units into a larger grouping; but for the present purpose it may be disregarded.

7. It has historical antecedents as old as Anglo-Saxon, where it sometimes sprang from the use of two words for one to meet the exigencies of translation from the Latin. It continued in Middle English, where native and Romance words could be used in pairs either for clarity or for emphasis.

8. P. 307. And see his analysis of it, pp. 308 f.

9. After scanning it, but without further attempt to study the rhythm,

he praises "the absolute perfection of rhythmical—never metrical—move-ment" and adds: "It has, I have said, never been surpassed. I sometimes doubt whether it has even been equalled" (pp. 162, 163). It is not, how-ever, among his selections from Donne in Craik's *English Prose*, II, 83 ff.

10. In the second edition Pater omitted "one," throwing the emphasis on "that."

CHAPTER VI

1. Mr. B. Dobrée confirms this with his question: "Why do we remem-ber, except for its insistence on rhythm, Milton's 'rousing herself like a strong man after sleep, and shaking her invincible locks'?" (p. 213) One answer would be—the boldness of the image. (See n. 3 below.)

2. T. F. Powys, *Mr. Weston's Good Wine*.

3. This does not represent Mr. Dobrée's writing at its best. It shows, however, some interesting revision of the original text of the lecture.

4. Cf. Middleton Murry, pp. 128 f. on these.

5. Saintsbury, p. 136.

6. Cf., especially on the position of adverbs, Aug. Western.

7. *Letters*, Bonchurch edition, XVIII, 107. In the same letter Swinburne mentioned Arnold's *Literature and Dogma*, and added in parentheses: "by the by I should have said there was more of *his* style than of mine traceable in Pater's." There is some point in this, but it is certain tricks of Arnold's style that Pater copied, not the rhythm.

8. Yet this paragraph of Pater's is not altogether perfect. Is "in every period" in its right place? Does not the second sentence trail needlessly after "in things"? Is not "methinks" too affected for the late nineteenth century? And is "something of its sting" quite free from a painful jingle? Or perhaps these are not preventible accidents, hinting still that we are all too late for a Golden Age, that our growth in intellectual delicacy has unmanned us for the simplicity of Numa's presence or of Numa's return.

9. I quote from the Bohn edition, 1893, v, 110 ff., except for the Windsor passage, which I quote from the 1803 edition.

10. Dr. Richards asks why no change may be made in Landor's sentence without disaster, but he can give only a partial answer, including this: "a very complex tide of neural settings, lowering the threshold for some kinds of stimuli and raising it for others" (p. 135)—which is helpful only to those who are on easy terms with a neural setting.

CHAPTER VII

1. These groups, sentence by sentence, are: 2, 4, 3. 4, 3, 2, 2. 4, 2, 2, 4. 5, 5. 3, 1, 1, 2, 1, 2. 2, 2, 3. 2, 3, 2, 3. 4, 4, 2, 3. 3, 3, 3, 3, 2, 4. 3, 1, 2, 5, 3, 2, 3, 2, 2, 2.

2. In the original text, in *Blackwood's*, the paragraph was much longer, but in his revision in 1854 DeQuincey altered very little the portion which he allowed to remain. The Roses and Fanny passage was unchanged.

3. James' style is of course not always such. He can write a long

sentence in the conventional forms of balance and parallelism; for example:

> There was none other, however, than the common and constant pressure,
> familiar to our friend under the rubric of *Postes et Télégraphes*—
>> the something in the air of these establishments;
>> the vibration of the vast strange life of the town,
>>> the influence of the types,
>>> the performers concocting their messages;
>> the little prompt Paris women,
>>> arranging, pretexting goodness knew what,
>>> driving the dreadful needle-pointed public pen
>>> at the dreadful sand-strewn public table:
>>>> implements that symbolized
>>>>> for Strether's too interpretative innocence
>>>> something more acute in manners,
>>>>> more sinister in morals,
>>>>> more fierce in the national life.

Bibliography

See also p. 222 on the *cursus*

Armstrong, Lilias E., and Ida C. Ward. *A Handbook of English Intonation.* Leipzig, 1926.

Arps, G. F., und O. Klemm. "Der Verlauf der Aufmerksamkeit bei rhythmischen Reizen," *Psychologische Studien,* IV (1909), 518-28.

Bolton, T. L. "Rhythm," *American Journal of Psychology,* VI (1894), 145-238.

Brown, Warner. *Time in English Verse Rhythm.* "Archives of Psychology," No. 10. New York, 1908.

———. "Temporal and Accentual Rhythm," *Psychological Review,* XVIII (1911), 336-46.

Clark, A. C. *Prose Rhythm in English.* Oxford, 1913.

Classe, André. *The Rhythm of English Prose.* Oxford, 1939.

Cooper, Lane. *Theories of Style.* New York, 1907.

Crandall, Irving B. *The Sounds of Speech.* New York, 1925.

Croll, Morris. "Attic Prose in the Seventeenth Century," *Studies in Philology,* XVIII (1921), 79-128.

———. "Attic Prose," *Shelling Anniversary Papers.* New York, 1923.

———. "Muret and the History of Attic Prose," PMLA, XXXIX (1924), 254-309.

Dobrée, Bonamy. *Modern Prose Style.* Oxford, 1934. For the lecture as first printed see the *Criterion,* July 1934.

Elton, Oliver. "English Prose Numbers," in *A Sheaf of Papers,* London, 1922, pp. 130-63. A revision of a paper in *Essays and Studies,* IV, 1913.

Emden, Cecil S. "Rhythmical Features in Dr. Johnson's Prose," *Review of English Studies,* XXV (1949), 38-54.

Fijn van Draat, P. *Rhythm in English Prose.* Heidelberg, 1910.

Fuhrken, G. L. *Standard English Speech.* Cambridge, 1932.

Graff, Willem L. *Language and Languages.* New York, 1932.

Griffith, Helen. *Time Patterns in Prose. A Study in Prose Rhythm Based upon Voice Records.* Princeton, 1929. "Psychological Monographs," No. 179.

Gropp, Friedrich. *Zur Ästhetik und statistischen Beschreibung des Prosa-Rhythmus.* Würzburg, 1915.

Gunn, J. Alexander. *The Problem of Time, an Historical and Critical Study.* London, [1929].

Hull, A. Eaglefield. *Modern Harmony. Its Explanation and Application.* London, n.d.

Jones, Daniel. *An Outline of English Phonetics,* 4th ed., New York, 1934.

Köhler, Wolfgang. *Gestalt Psychology.* New York, 1929.

Lanz, Henry. *The Physical Basis of Rime.* Palo Alto, Calif. 1931.

Landry, Eugène. *La théorie du rythme et le rythme du français déclamé.* Paris, 1911.

Limouze, A. Sanford. "A Note on Vergil and *The Battle of the Books,*" *Philological Quarterly,* xxvi (1948), 85-89.

Lipsky, Abram. *Rhythm as a Distinguishing Characteristic of Prose Style.* New York, 1907.

Lotspeich, C. M. "Poetry, Prose, and Rhythm," PMLA, xxxvii (1922), 293-310.

MacColl, D. S. "Rhythm in English Verse, Prose, and Speech," *Essays and Studies,* v (1914), 7-50.

Mason, John. *An Essay on the Power and Harmony of Prosaic Numbers.* London, 1749.

MacDougall, Robert. "The Structure of Simple Rhythm Forms," *Harvard Psychological Studies,* i (1903), 309 ff.

————. "Rhythm, Time and Number," *American Journal of Psychology,* xiii (1902), 88-97.

Miller, D. C. *The Science of Musical Sounds.* New York, 1916.

Morris, Amos R. "Liddell's Laws of English Rhythm," *Papers of the Michigan Academy of Science, Arts and Letters,* xxii (1936), 485-91.

Murry, J. Middleton. *The Problem of Style.* Oxford, 1922.

Ogden, R. M. "The Attributes of Sound," *Psychological Review*, xxv (1918), 227-41.

Paget, Violet [Vernon Lee]. "Studies in Literary Psychology," in *The Handling of Words*. London, 1923.

Patterson, W. M. *The Rhythm of Prose*. New York, 1917.

Pike, Kenneth L. *The Intonation of American Speech*. Ann Arbor, 1946.

Prall, D. W. *Aesthetic Analysis*. New York, 1936.

Read, Herbert. *English Prose Style*. London, 1928.

Richards, I. A. *Principles of Literary Criticism*. New York, 1924.

Ross, F. B. "The Measurement of Time-Sense as an Element in the Sense of Rhythm," *Psychological Monographs*. "University of Iowa Studies in Psychology." Iowa City, 1914.

Ruckmich, Christian A. *"The Rôle of Kinaesthesis in the Perception of Rhythm,"* American Journal of Psychology, xxiv (1913), 305-59.

Saintsbury, George. *A History of English Prose Rhythm*. London, 1912; 1922.

Schmidt, Wolfgang. "Satzsinn und Tonfall," *Anglia*, LXI (1937), 98-111.

Schubiger, Maria. *The Role of Intonation in Spoken English*. Cambridge, 1935.

Scott, F. N. "The Most Fundamental Differentia on Poetry and Prose," PMLA, xix (1904), 258 ff.

———. "The Scansion of Prose Rhythm," PMLA, xx (1905), 207 ff.

Scott, J. H., and Zilpha E. Chandler. *Phrasal Patterns in English Prose*. New York, [1932].

Sears, Charles H. "A Contribution to the Psychology of Rhythm," *American Journal of Psychology*, xiii (1902), 28-61.

Sonnenschein, E. A. *What Is Rhythm? An Essay*. Oxford, 1925.

Snell, Ada. *Pause. A Study of the Nature and Rhythmical Function in Verse*. Ann Arbor, 1918.

Strecker, Karl. *Introduction à l'Etude de latin médiéval*, trad. Paul van de Woestijne. Gand, 1933.

Sturtevant, Edgar H. *An Introduction to Linguistic Science.* New Haven, 1947.

Swadesh, Morris. "On the Analysis of English Syllabics," *Language*, XXIII (1947), 137-50.

Taig, Thomas. *Rhythm and Metre.* Cardiff, 1929.

Tempest, Norton R. *The Rhythm of English Prose.* Cambridge, 1930.

Thomson, William. *The Rhythm of Speech.* Glasgow, 1907.

Wallin, J. E. W. "[Three] Experimental Studies of Rhythm and Time," *Psychological Review*, XVIII (1911), 100-131, 202-22; XIX (1912), 271-98.

———. *Researches on the Rhythm of Speech.* "Studies from the Yale Psychological Laboratory," No. 9. New Haven, 1901.

Western, August. *On Sentence-Rhythm and Word-Order in Modern English.* Christiania, 1908.

Whitehead, A. N. *An Enquiry concerning the Principles of Natural Knowledge.* Cambridge, 1919.

Williams, C. F. Abdy. *The Aristoxenian Theory of Musical Rhythm.* Cambridge, 1911.

———. *The Rhythm of Modern Music.* London, 1909.

Wimsatt, W. K., Jr. *The Prose Style of Samuel Johnson.* New Haven, 1941.

Woodrow, Herbert. *A Quantitative Study of Rhythm.* "Archives of Psychology," No. 14. New York, 1909.

———. "The Rôle of Pitch in Rhythm," *Psychological Review*, XVIII (1911), 54-77.